The Essential Home Buyer's Checklists

Denise L. Evans
Attorney at Law

SPHINX® PUBLISHING
AN IMPRINT OF SOURCEBOOKS, INC.®
NAPERVILLE, ILLINOIS
www.SphinxLegal.com

First Edition: 2007

Published by: **Sphinx® Publishing, An Imprint of Sourcebooks, Inc.®**

Naperville Office
P.O. Box 4410
Naperville, Illinois 60567-4410
630-961-3900
Fax: 630-961-2168
www.sourcebooks.com
www.SphinxLegal.com

This publication is designed to provide accurate and authoritative information in regard
to the subject matter covered. It is sold with the understanding that the publisher is not
engaged in rendering legal, accounting, or other professional service. If legal advice or
other expert assistance is required, the services of a competent professional person should
be sought.

*From a Declaration of Principles Jointly Adopted by a Committee of
the American Bar Association and a Committee of Publishers and Associations*

This product is not a substitute for legal advice.

Disclaimer required by Texas statutes.

Library of Congress Cataloging-in-Publication Data
Evans, Denise L.
  The essential home buyer's checklists : 140 best ways to avoid the costly
mistakes and hidden dangers every home buyer must face / by Denise L. Evans.
    p. cm.
  Includes index.
  ISBN-13: 978-1-57248-559-4 (pbk. : alk. paper)
  ISBN-10: 1-57248-559-0 (pbk. : alk. paper)
  1. House buying--United States--Handbooks, manuals, etc. 2. Residential
real estate--Purchasing--United States--Handbooks, manuals, etc. I. Title.

HD255.E95 2006
643'.120973--dc22
                                                              2006030262

Printed and bound in the United States of America.
SB — 10 9 8 7 6 5 4 3 2 1

Contents

Section III: Construction

Section IV: Contracts

Section VI: Moving

Introduction

Welcome to an exciting adventure—the purchase of your new home! Consider me your tour guide, pointing out important landmarks along the way and resources you can use for greater depth of knowledge on particular subjects.

The checklists in this book are designed to get your attention and offer a small amount of information on each item. Many ideas will prompt you to think of additional things. That's terrific, because no one author can cover all the ground necessary for such a vast subject.

It's also almost impossible to give advice that's right for the entire country. Every single state has minor legal differences, usually pertaining to technicalities. With that in mind, always check with a local attorney before writing a contract, signing a contract, or embarking on some unusual strategy. If you think I've overlooked something important, or if you have a comment or question, get in touch with me. I promise I'll answer. You can reach me at checklists@deniselevans.com.

   With that little bit of housekeeping out of the way, charge ahead for the rest of the book. You'll find insider real estate tricks, sound advice, explanations of how things work in the real world, and tons of commonsense tips not found anyplace else. When you're finished reading, you'll feel like a real estate expert yourself, ready to tackle anything.

Section I:
Finances

Chapter 1:

Deciding How Much Home You Can Afford

Your new home search should begin by asking yourself the tough question: "How much can I really afford?" Nearly everyone can find a way to afford comfortable housing in a safe neighborhood with the features that are most important to them—school quality, ease of commuting, leisure activities, status, distance to (or away from) relatives, or whatever else they desire. It's not always easy, but it is a great adventure with a fabulous prize at the end. It is important to remember that the answer to the question of how much you can afford is usually a different number than how much the salesperson at the mortgage company is willing to loan you. Set realistic goals for yourself by taking the following steps.

- ☑ Examine how you spend your money now
- ☑ Think about how your finances might change
- ☑ Anticipate changes after a home purchase
- ☑ Prepare a housing budget
- ☑ Translate mortgage payment into maximum loan amount
- ☑ Improve your odds if finances are a problem

☑ Examine how you spend your money now

☑ Gather all your credit card statements for the last year
☑ Print out or collect all check registers for the past year
☑ Make a list of items you normally purchase with cash
☑ Calculate your average monthly take-home pay

You need to figure out where it all goes every month. It's not enough to take the money you spend on rent and use the magic of math to translate it into a possible purchase price. Life's not that simple. Some expenses will go up, some will come down, and whole categories of expenses will surprise you.

After examining your spending patterns, you might discover that you eat out all the time because your apartment is too small to entertain and too boring to endure by yourself. Owning a home could change all that and reward you with substantial cash savings!

On the other hand, a prestigious home in a status neighborhood will cost more than the mortgage payments—you'll be expected to have nice furniture, participate in community activities, entertain the neighbors, and maintain the lawn in an acceptable manner. Do you have something similar going on already, or will this require additional money in the budget? You won't know until you start with the baseline question: how do you spend your money now?

☑ Gather all your credit card statements for the last year

One of the easiest ways to figure out how you are actually spending your money is to gather all of your credit card statements for the past twelve months. If your computer or credit card companies categorize your expenses for you, great! If not, start separating your purchases into areas such as the following. If you need more categories, add them.

- ☑ Alcohol/tobacco
- ☑ Books/magazines
- ☑ Clothing/jewelry
- ☑ Credit card interest
- ☑ Decorating
- ☑ Dining out
- ☑ Education
- ☑ Entertainment
- ☑ Fitness
- ☑ Gas
- ☑ Groceries
- ☑ Hobbies
- ☑ Impulse purchases

- ☑ Laundry/dry cleaning
- ☑ Membership dues
- ☑ Routine auto maintenance
- ☑ Routine health care
- ☑ Services (Internet, Sirius, XM Radio, Onstar, NetFlix)
- ☑ Sports
- ☑ Storage rent
- ☑ Travel
- ☑ Miscellaneous
- ☑ Other:
- ☑ Other:
- ☑ Other:

It's not so important to figure out the exact category for something, as long as you are reasonably close and consistent. Don't worry about whether dinner and a movie goes under "dining out" or "entertainment," or should be divided between the two. Pick something and stick with it.

Try to avoid overanalyzing expenses—you'll get bogged down in the details and quit, losing the value of this exercise.

☑ Print out or collect all check registers for the past year

The next step is to do the same categorization with checks you write. Make sure you include debit card purchases. Possible categories could duplicate those on the credit card list, in addition to the following.

☑ Auto insurance	☑ Loan #1:
☑ Auto payments	☑ Loan #2:
☑ Auto repairs	☑ Mass transportation
☑ Charity	☑ Parental support
☑ Child care	☑ Rent
☑ Child support/alimony	☑ Renter's insurance
☑ Credit card interest & fees	☑ Utilities
☑ Furniture rental	☑ Miscellaneous
☑ Health insurance	☑ Other:
☑ Insurance deductibles	☑ Other:
☑ Investments	☑ Other:

☑ Make a list of items you normally purchase with cash

Give it your best educated guess regarding how much you spend in the following areas or others that might apply to you. When in doubt, take notes for a week or two to get a better idea of what you spend.

☑ Charity	☑ Newspapers
☑ Coffee/beverages	☑ Snacks
☑ Fast food	☑ Tobacco products
☑ Lottery/gambling	☑ Other:

Be sure to cross-reference the credit card and check categories for other items. If you spend over $15 a week on a regular basis for something, assign a category name to it and write it down.

Putting these lists together shouldn't take too much effort, and in the end you have a realistic picture of how you are spending your money. The last thing you need to do is determine how much money you have coming in every month.

☑ Calculate your average monthly take-home pay

It is fairly easy to calculate your average monthly take-home pay if you have a regular job with predictable income. It's a little bit more complicated for those who work on commission, own their own business, or otherwise have money coming in unpredictable amounts at unreliable times. How much can you absolutely depend on, month in and month out? What additional money will you earn during the year (after taxes), and how often will you receive it? Is there other money you rely on, such as investment income, child support, alimony, long-term disability payments, trust funds, or prize money? You may need to set up some sort of savings or investment account to cover mortgage payments during the lean months.

☑ Think about how your finances might change

☑ What additional income can you count on?

☑ Will your net income decrease, and if so, by how much?

☑ How can you cut down on your expenses?

☑ Are you currently saving for a down payment?

Gathering the previous information is great (and necessary), but it means nothing if either your income or expenses are about to have a drastic change. If that is a possibility, then you need to look at a couple of things.

☑ What additional income can you count on?

Do you receive a cost-of-living raise each year? Did Aunt Tillie die and leave you some rental property, but the estate has to clear probate before you'll get it? Will you receive a large tax refund this year? If you know that some additional money will be coming your way soon—for sure—write down how much additional money you can expect each month and then subtract something for taxes, depending on your bracket.

☑ Will your net income decrease, and if so, by how much?

No, it's not pleasant, but if you know an income decrease is coming, it has to be faced. Divorce could result in alimony, periodic property settlement payments, and child support. In addition, income-producing property might be given to your ex-spouse. Your employer may have plans to shift some health insurance costs to employees, increase the deductibles or co-pay amounts, or cut overtime pay. You may also have student loans that are kicking in.

Write down the things you know will change, and how much they will affect your income. Just to be cautious, also write down things that seem fairly certain according to the rumor mill. If they'll have a dramatic impact on your ability to make mortgage payments, factor them into your calculations or don't buy anything until you see what happens.

☑ How can you cut down your expenses?

Be reasonable when thinking about how you can cut down expenses. You are not going to live on dried beans and canned vegetables for the next three years. You might cut your entertainment and clothing budget in half, though. This is relatively painless with a little planning. Buy discounted clothing at season-end for the next year, or shop consignment stores. Join a mail-order DVD rental club instead of going out to movies. Take advantage of free wine tastings at local stores for a fun experience and a chance to meet new people. Find out how to be a secret shopper for restaurants so you can eat for free and receive payment. Travel to state parks (many of which have excellent hotel and recreational facilities) instead of taking resort vacations. With enough motivation—such as owning a new home—you'll be surprised how much money you can save.

☑ Are you currently saving for a down payment?

You won't need to save that money each month after a purchase, so it's an expense that will go down. You'll still need to save something for emergencies and retirement, but not at the same rate as before.

Remember, it's okay for a portion of your investments to be in your home.

☑ Anticipate changes after a home purchase

After you buy a new home, how your money will be spent will change. Most of these changes will be new expenses, but some might actually decrease. If you move from a suburban apartment to a downtown loft, you'll see dramatic reductions in your auto expenses—unless you keep your car and also have to pay for monthly parking. The following list includes some things to think about. Be sure to factor in equipment purchases, such as a lawn mower or snowblower. Some things provided free by friends or relatives may have to be replaced if you move elsewhere, such as baby-sitting and day care services. Also, certain things that are free or discounted in an apartment—such as Internet and trash pickup—will cost you in a house.

- ☑ Lawn care
- ☑ Snow removal
- ☑ Pest control
- ☑ Exterior painting
- ☑ Pool maintenance
- ☑ Condo fees
- ☑ Co-op rent
- ☑ Neighborhood association
- ☑ Child care
- ☑ Commuting
- ☑ Second car for spouse
- ☑ House repairs
- ☑ Water and trash pickup
- ☑ Cable television
- ☑ High-speed Internet
- ☑ Recreational and work-out facilities

Also remember that if your desire to buy a new home is because of a planned or current pregnancy, then you'll have new expenses associated with your child. Be sure to include amounts for disposable diapers, formula, day care, life insurance, and increased health care costs. Of course, if it's a first child in the family, the grandparents will usually cover you with clothing, toys, and furniture—so don't worry about that.

☑ Prepare a housing budget

You have put a lot of time into gathering financial information. Now you need to convert that data into a number you can use to make some real decisions. To prepare your housing budget, take your after-tax income (take-home pay), and subtract the living expenses you have already calculated, leaving out what you currently pay for rent. The answer is the maximum amount you can afford to spend each month for mortgage payments, insurance, and real estate taxes. Lenders usually collect a monthly reserve for annual insurance premiums and real estate taxes. They may or may not also collect for school taxes, fire district taxes, and library taxes. Some governments charge separately for those items, some don't charge at all, and others bill everything together in the property taxes. If it's not a monthly expense, you will have to come up with the yearly amount in one or two payments, so add it to your monthly expense calculations to avoid a crunch when a bill comes.

For the time being, assume that your whole housing budget can be used for mortgage payments. Taxes and insurance will vary widely depending on your jurisdiction and the size, type, and location of your home, but this number is a good starting point.

☑ Translate mortgage payment into maximum loan amount

You have done a lot to figure out what you can spend each month on your new home, but when doing your search, you want to know how much you can afford in terms of your maximum loan amount. To calculate this, convert your housing budget number into a loan amount. This is fairly simple. You can go to any number of websites, such as **www.cheapskatemonthly.com**, to find calculators that will do the work for you, or you can call a lender or mortgage broker and ask. Be sure to stress that you don't want to prequalify for a loan at the present time—you just want them to help you with a math problem. You can also figure the number for yourself on your home computer.

This amount is the maximum loan you can afford. How much home this money will buy will depend on the size of your down payment as well as the amount your budget will decrease because of taxes and insurance. It's a starting point, though. If the maximum loan amount you can afford is not enough to purchase housing—even with 100% financing, free taxes, and free insurance—then it's time to do some creative thinking, earn more money, trim out some expenses, or all three.

Use Microsoft Excel to create your own mortgage calculator.

◇	A	B	
1	2000	Monthly Payment	
2	7.25	Interest Rate	
3	30	Years in Mortgage	
4	=PV(A2/100/12,A3*12,-A1)	Formula to Give Loan Amount	
5			
6			
7			

In cell A1, put the monthly payment you can afford (such as 2,000).

In cell A2, put the annual interest rate (such as 7.25). You can find the going interest rates in your area in your local paper or by calling a local bank.

In cell A3, put the number of years you want on your mortgage term (such as 30).

Don't rearrange the order of these numbers.

In cell A4, write the following formula *exactly*; as it appears. There are no spaces, and that's a minus sign in front of A1. Don't enter numbers—just the cell addresses of A1, A2, and A3.

$$=PV(A2/100/12,A3*12,-A1)$$

Now, based on what you put in the payment, interest, and term fields, A4 will tell you how much of a mortgage loan those numbers translate to.

For the above example, the answer is $293,179.35. See if you obtain the same answer. If so, the spreadsheet you created is correct.

☑ Improve your odds if finances are a problem

☑ Search for rehab projects at below-market prices

☑ Shop for a duplex, small apartment building (four units), or something with a garage apartment

☑ Concentrate on foreclosure properties

☑ Limit your shopping to properties owned by sellers who will hold the financing

☑ Search for government subsidized home ownership programs

☑ Buy land, and then buy a home from a demolition site and have it moved to your property

☑ Talk to all of your friends, read everything you can read, and think creatively and expansively

If your monthly income won't support the mortgage payments for the kind of home you'd like to buy, engage in *possibility thinking*. This goes beyond the boring stuff, such as making more money or spending less. These things work and are important, but there are other things you can do to become a home owner.

☑ Search for rehab projects at below-market prices

You don't have to be handy. A simple coat of paint and a few flowers will do wonders for many properties. Rip out old cabinets and replace them with free-standing cabinetry you got at the flea market. Steam-clean ancient carpeting and cover it with area rugs if it's clean but still ugly. Hire professional roofers, plumbers, and electricians unless you know what you're doing. You could have an old-fashioned barn raising—invite some talented friends over to do the technical work and turn the whole thing into a party.

☑ Shop for a duplex, small apartment building (four units), or something with a garage apartment

The rental income you can get from the other units will subsidize your mortgage payments. Plus, with these buildings, it is often easier to obtain financing, as these will be treated as commercial loans rather than consumer loans. Even if you must live in the garage apartment and rent out the house, the property will be yours. As your finances improve, you'll be able to reverse the living arrangement.

☑ Concentrate on foreclosure properties

Foreclosed properties can often be purchased at substantial savings with attractive financing terms. For more guidance on this subject, buy my book, *How To Make Money On Foreclosures*.

☑ Limit your shopping to properties owned by sellers who will hold the financing

You can obtain below-market interest rates in these situations, which might get the mortgage payments down to an affordable number.

☑ Search for government subsidized home ownership programs

Your city or town planning department can tell you about low interest rate loans for buying in a revitalization district. The U.S. Department of Housing and Urban Development (**www.hud.gov**) has special home ownership programs, including *Teacher Next Door* and *Officer Next Door*. These two offer foreclosed homes to qualifying buyers at a 50% discount with nearly 100% financing. Search for these, or similar, incentive programs.

☑ **Buy land, and then buy a home from a demolition site and have it moved to your property**

Many perfectly good houses are located on land taken by eminent domain or purchased for shopping centers or other development. It's a significant expense to demolish the homes and dispose of the rubbish, which is why they're usually offered for sale at bargain-basement prices.

☑ **Talk to all your friends, read everything you can read, and think creatively and expansively**

Nothing will keep you from buying your first home soon, if you set your mind to it.

Chapter 2:
Credit Scores and Credit Repair

When you converted your housing budget into your maximum loan amount, you did so by guessing what your interest rate would be. The thing that will have the greatest impact on what your interest rate will be is your credit score.

Finding out, tracking, and possibly repairing your credit score are some of the first things you should do. A great score will qualify you for the lowest interest rates. This will lower your monthly payments, meaning you can afford more home than you might think.

A terrible score can be repaired, but it will take time. Fortunately, repairing your credit score is a multitask item, and most of the work occurs with the passage of time. While you are house hunting, you can also be taking steps to repair your credit (should it be an issue).

☑ Obtain and improve your credit score

☑ Obtain and improve your credit score

    ☑ Find out target credit scores for lenders
    ☑ Order credit reports from all three agencies
    ☑ Beware of fraud
    ☑ Order and track your credit score
    ☑ Maintain good credit
    ☑ Improve your score

☑ Find out target credit scores for lenders

Today, the home loan market is very competitive. In order to be as efficient as possible, lenders cannot afford the luxury of the time it takes getting to know you personally to make judgments on whether you will repay the loan. Instead, lenders rely on third parties to evaluate your strength as a borrower, which they do by assigning you a credit score. This is why credit scores are much more important than they used to be.

Scores of 650 or more will qualify you for the best interest rates. Scores of 750 or above are considered excellent, while scores of 800 or higher are star-quality credit ratings. The higher your score, the more leeway you'll be given if you don't meet other underwriting guidelines for income, job stability, or loan-to-value ratios.

Don't give up if your score is under 650—you can always take steps to improve it, or you can find financing from a lender that specializes in what are called *B-paper* or *B-loans* (as in, A-quality, B-quality, etc.). The interest rates will be higher and the fees will usually be larger, but you can qualify for a loan.

The beginning point is to find out what scores different lenders look for. Most will not advertise this information anywhere. You will need to make phone calls to find out the *target scores* for their different loan programs. Every company is different, so be sure to call several lenders if you have any doubts about your qualifications.

☑ Order credit reports from all three agencies

Almost all lenders use at least one of the three major credit reporting agencies—Experian, Equifax, or TransUnion. By law, all three agencies must give you one free credit report per year, but you can request (and pay for) more than one. For details, go to **www.annualcreditreport.com** or call 877-322-8228. This is the federally mandated website and toll-free number for credit reports.

You can also write to:

Annual Credit Report Request Service
P.O. Box 105283
Atlanta, GA 30348

Don't be fooled by the website **www.freecreditreport.com**—that's not the official site.

Obtain a report from each agency, as they will all be a little bit different from each other. Requesting your own credit report will not reduce your score.

Your credit reports will contain a large amount of personal information, in addition to data about your debts and payment history. Read all of it very carefully in order to confirm the accuracy of the report. Addresses or debts you don't recognize may be signs of identity theft. Other items may contain mistakes that can be corrected. If your report contains negative information that is accurate, verify its date. Negative data must be omitted by federal law if it is too old to report. (The section "Improve Your Score" on page 22 will tell you more about how to get that information removed.)

☑ Beware of fraud

There are many Internet and other scams offering to provide you with free credit reports. Use only the website, the address, or the phone number listed on page 19. Never link to something from an email or other website. Always make sure you are putting in the exact address—**www.annualcreditreport.com**—into your navigation bar. Criminals are able to make it look like you are linking to this website, when you are really being directed to a location that will steal your Social Security number and other identity information.

☑ Order and track your credit score

The law does not require credit reporting agencies to give you a free copy of your *credit score*, just the report. You'll have to pay to obtain the score, but the cost is minor. Use the same contact information as you did for ordering a credit report. Credit scores change almost daily, depending on what information is being reported and how it affects the scoring equation. If you have any fears about having a low or borderline score, then pay for a monthly or annual service that gives you updated access as often as you like.

Some of those packages of services include "what if" calculators—how would your score change if you did certain things, such as paying down credit cards or paying off collection accounts. They can prove to be invaluable.

☑ Maintain good credit

☑ Even a good credit score might be temporary. Don't take chances with this! Follow this advice to maintain your advantage.

☑ Pay all bills on time. If you can't do that, for some reason, at least pay the ones that report to the credit reporting agencies. If you can't do that, for some reason, at least pay the ones that report to the credit reporting agencies. Examples include credit cards and car, bank, or finance company loans. See who currently appears on your credit report. Keep them happy! Even if you have questions about a medical bill, pay it within ninety days or make arrangements for a payment plan. Most health care providers turn their bills over to collection agencies after a very short time, and this will appear on your report.

☑ Don't get any more credit cards. This includes store cards that offer you instant discounts if you apply. Also, avoid moving balances to new cards in order to obtain low introductory interest rates. While both of these things may save you some money immediately, they will lower your score, making your interest rate for a mortgage go up.

☑ Do not fill out any formal applications or allow anyone to obtain credit reports until right before you're ready to borrow the money. When loan shopping, tell lenders your credit score and some general financial information, and then ask them what rates and terms you qualify for. Credit inquiries made over the course of a short time—usually two weeks—seems to show that you're shopping and doesn't reduce your score. Many inquiries over a long period of time tells the scoring computer that you can't get approved anywhere. That might be inaccurate, but you can't change your score by providing a good explanation of your actions. The computer doesn't care.

☑ Improve your score

Resist the urge to immediately find a credit repair consultant and pay him or her money. Many engage in illegal activities.

How it works in the real world: Credit Repair

Some credit repair companies know the law and take advantage of human errors. They know that if you contest something as incorrect, the credit grantor has only thirty days to confirm its accuracy. If the creditor misses the deadline, the bad credit information must be removed. A large number of credit repair companies advise you to fraudulently contest all adverse credit information in the hopes that some will be deleted because of timing problems. This is illegal.

Other companies, while honest and reputable, charge expensive fees for the same information you're receiving here for the price of a book. There's nothing secret or difficult about improving your score. Follow a few simple guidelines and you'll see dramatic changes fairly soon.

Recent credit information has more weight than older stuff. Paying bills on time each month is much more important than paying off old debts in their entirety.

Paying off credit card balances entirely will raise your score a little bit. Being patient and making large monthly payments over the course of six to twelve months will increase your score dramatically. Your credit score is all about how you pay your bills each and every month. The scoring computer is not impressed by people who go deeply into debt, come into periodic windfalls of cash and then pay everyone in full.

Correct all mistakes on your credit report. If you contest an item, the credit reporting agency must request verification from the credit grantor. Failure to confirm that data within thirty days will result in its deletion.

You should request deletion of any information that is too old to be legally reported, even if it is accurate. *There is nothing illegal or unethical about this.* The rules can be found in the Federal Code, at 15 U.S.C. §1681, or online at the website of the Government Printing Office, at **www.gpoaccess.gov/uscode**. On the website, enter "15usc1681c" (without the quotes) in the search box under "2000 Edition, Supplement 2." This will take you to the rules. According to law, the following items cannot be reported, and must be deleted if you contest them.

☑ Civil suits, civil judgments, or arrest records older than ten years or the statute of limitations, whichever is longer.

☑ Paid tax liens older than seven years. (Note: Credit reporting bureaus and the Federal Trade Commission, which administers the rules, take the position that *unpaid* tax liens can be reported forever. This seems to be against the plain language of the statute, but arguing will get you nowhere.)

☑ Accounts placed for collection more than seven years ago. When in doubt, the FTC assumes that an account will be placed for collection 180 days after it first becomes delinquent.

☑ Anything else, other than crimes, older than seven years.

☑ An important exception allows reporting of older information if the consumer is applying for a loan of $150,000 or more, life insurance with a face value of $150,000 or more, or a job with an annual salary of $75,000 or more. If you're borderline and have some old adverse credit information, you might want to increase your down payment in order to reduce the loan below $150,000.

For More Information

Most colleges, universities, community colleges, and chambers of commerce offer regular seminars on credit-related issues. There are also numerous books focused on the subject.

If you have Internet access, all three credit reporting agencies have excellent information about credit reports and scoring. Visit **www.annualcreditreport.com** and follow the links to these sites. The Federal Trade Commission has a great website at **www.ftc.gov/credit**. Search the Internet with caution, though. Most of the credit repair companies pay for good placement when you search on their terms. Include the words "university," "magazine," or "beware" to find useful articles and avoid a lot of the advertising. You can also call the Federal Trade Commission (FTC) at 877-382-4357, or write to:

Consumer Response Center
Federal Trade Commission
600 Pennsylvania, NW
H-130
Washington, DC 20580

You should request copies of the following pamphlets from the FTC.

☑ Credit and Your Consumer Rights
☑ Getting Credit: What You Need to Know About Your Credit
☑ Building a Better Credit Report
☑ Credit Scoring
☑ How to Dispute Credit Report Errors

The best defense against fraud, unethical practices, or exclusion from the American dream of home ownership is to be an informed consumer.

Chapter 3:
Shopping for Financing

Lenders and mortgage brokers offer a wide variety of loan programs and interest rates. You may also qualify for some government programs, or you may find a seller willing to hold the financing for you. All the options can get confusing unless you have a plan. If you'd like to start with a better all-around education about financing options, check out Appendix B, "Crash Course on Financing."

To prepare for your home loan, take the following steps.

- ☑ **Know your credit score**
- ☑ **Prepare a request for proposal**
- ☑ **Start collecting financial information about yourself**
- ☑ **Learn about special assistance programs**
- ☑ **Stay knowledgeable about expected rate changes**
- ☑ **Beware of add-on fees and discount points**
- ☑ **Plan ahead to avoid PMI charges**
- ☑ **Always ask if a seller will hold the financing**

☑ Know your credit score

You've done your homework, and now you are ready to get your loan. Shopping for financing is more tedious than difficult, but everything you have done in preparation will make meeting with lenders go much more smoothly. If you haven't done so already, find out your credit score. Even if it's not terrific, it's important to be absolutely honest about your score when shopping for financing. Remember, lenders are in a very competitive business. They are not going to remember a poor score and hold it against you if you later improve it. They want to loan you money. Beware, though, of the ones who make you think your low credit score disqualifies you from any reasonable interest rates. Your less-than-terrific score may be just enough for low interest rates. That's why you want to shop for financing and obtain several different opinions, rather than take the chance of getting the wrong lender.

How it works in the real world: Perspective

When making buying decisions for a home and financing, don't think solely in terms of honesty or trust. Different people will give you different advice, depending on their perspective. Remember, a surgeon usually thinks surgery will fix your health problems, a drug company thinks drugs will do the trick, and your grandmother has always cured her ails with herb tea. None of them lack integrity, but each simply gives advice from his or her own life's experiences. Even an honest mortgage broker who specializes in finding lenders for people with poor credit may be unaware that your borderline credit score might be enough for cheaper financing. Always obtain second and third opinions.

☑ Prepare a request for proposal

Shopping for financing is one of those really important chores that almost cries out for something in writing. The field is just too complicated and it is too difficult to remember all the ins and outs to leave it to faulty memory. In addition, lenders like to quote their terms in different ways that make it difficult to compare apples to apples. One might say, "We can offer you prime plus 2" and another might say "Our interest rate is 250 basis points over LIBOR." Another might offer a low interest rate but high up-front fees and expenses. Do you want to figure that out? With a *Request for Proposal* (RFP), they have to put down all the information in terms you can understand. A sample, with the information you would complete in italics and blanks for the information the lender should complete, is on page 28.

Keep all of the responses in a file folder. When it's time to make a final decision, recheck your credit score and visit with the three most promising lenders or brokers to update their quotes. If your credit score is at all marginal, apply with all three simultaneously. It will not affect your credit score if done at the same time.

Request for Proposal for Financing

Date: *January 1, 2007*
To: *First National Mortgage Company*

    You are being asked to complete a written quote for financing to purchase a home in the approximate amount of *$175,000.* I understand that your quote is subject to underwriting, and that rates or terms may change by the time I wish to secure financing. This quote is for initial evaluation only. My current credit score is *680.* I want to [choose all that apply] *obtain the maximum amount possible, keep my payments as low as possible, and/or make a down payment of 20% of the price.* If I can secure better terms with a better credit score, please indicate here your target score _____, and provide a separate quote for terms at that score.

Amount financed: _____

Current interest rate: _____%

Adjustable or fixed rate: _____

Amortization period: _____

Rate lock good for _____ days

How much is the fee for a rate lock? _____

Balloon or rate changes when? _____

Monthly payments: _____

Total amount for all lender fees: $ _____

Additional amounts to be included in monthly payments: $_____

Is PMI insurance required, and what are the charges? _____

Identify all anticipated third-party fees and expenses, and approximate amount: _____

Why should I choose you for my borrowing needs?

☑ Start collecting financial information about yourself

The loan application process will require a good bit of information from you. If you start collecting it now, while things are relatively calm, you'll have a better chance of getting the best financing terms possible. Using whatever system works best for you—a file folder, a shoe box, a special drawer in the kitchen for all house-buying stuff—begin getting your information together. Depending on the lender, you'll need some or all of the following things:

☑ tax returns for the last three years;

☑ W-2s from last year, if you haven't filed a return yet;

☑ proof of sources and amounts of other income (such as alimony);

☑ name, contact info, account numbers, balances, and monthly payments for other lenders and credit card issuers;

☑ name and contact info for credit references if you have little credit history (landlords and utilities are good references);

☑ a monthly budget, before purchase, of all income and expenses; and,

☑ proof of any explanations about bad credit information in your file.

☑ Learn about special assistance programs

Before going to a lender, find out all you can about any special assistance programs that may be available to you. Low-income housing assistance is available from a number of federal, state, and local agencies. Programs might include low interest rate loans, interest-free down payment loans, or special pricing for qualified buyers of government-owned properties. The Department of Housing and Urban Development (HUD) sells some foreclosed homes at discounts to teachers and law enforcement personnel who live in the neighborhoods they serve. There are Native American programs, assistance for widows and orphans of armed services personnel, and incentives for moving to rural or inner-city areas. The Internet will be your best source of information. Mortgage brokers are often knowledgeable about these programs. Local HUD or USDA offices can also help with information or leads to other resources. To start, go to **www.hud.gov** or call 800-569-4287 for a referral to a housing counselor in your area. Refer to Appendix B for more information.

☑ Stay knowledgeable about expected rate changes

You may need to move quickly if interest rates are expected to increase dramatically in the near future. Follow the news articles on this subject, and stay in touch with lenders and mortgage brokers. It may be necessary to speed up your house hunting if there's an anticipated rate change. On the other hand, don't get carried away and sacrifice important inspections or other such things in the name of speed. On a $175,000 loan, a rate change from 7% to 7¼% for a thirty-year mortgage will increase your monthly payments only $29.53.

☑ Beware of add-on fees and discount points

Lenders sometimes charge *origination points*, or a certain percentage of the loan, as an add-on expense. One point is equal to 1% of the loan. Out of that money, they might pay some third-party expenses, such as an appraisal fee, or the whole thing might be pure profit. Make sure you find out what the points cover. This is a highly negotiable item.

It's a little confusing, but there's another kind of point. Lenders will offer you *discount points* equal to 1% of the loan in order to reduce the interest rate on your loan. What you are buying with it is a cheaper interest rate than what is offered to John Q. Public. The lender might tell you that you can reduce your interest rate by ¼% if you pay one point. It sounds enticing, but it rarely works out well.

It almost never makes sense to pay discount points—you usually have to own your home at least five to seven years in order to realize any true savings. Here's an example of what would happen if you could pay one point and lower your interest rate ¼%.

$175,000 loan, 30 years, 6½% interest is equal to monthly payments of:	$1,106.12
Payment of one point for a $175,000 loan is equal to up-front payment of:	$1,750.00
Same loan at 6¼% interest is equal to monthly payments of:	$1,077.51
Monthly savings if you pay one point:	$28.61
Number of months of $28.61 savings to equal $1,750.00:	61 months (5 years)

Other fees, such as underwriting, review appraisal, credit review, and so on, can be very high. These fees are also negotiable, and most of them should be waived. Many commentators call these *junk fees*.

☑ Plan ahead to avoid PMI charges

Private mortgage insurance (PMI) is often required by lenders if you pay less than a 20% down payment on your home. It protects the lender in case you default, but you are the one to pay the premiums. On a $100,000 home with only 10% down, the fee can be around $40 per month or higher. This can really add up over time. By law, the insurance must be automatically cancelled when you pay your loan down to 78% of the original appraised value, but there are many loopholes that allow it to continue longer. On the previous example, if you borrow $90,000 at 7% interest, it will take ten years before your balance is low enough for PMI to drop off. You're better off finding a less expensive home or deferring purchase long enough to save the money you need for a 20% down payment.

For more information about PMI insurance, visit the website of the Federal Trade Commission at **www.ftc.gov/bcp/ conline/pubs/alerts/pmialrt.htm**, or call 877-382-4367 and ask for the pamphlet entitled, "Cancellation of Private Mortgage Insurance: Federal Law May Save You Hundreds of Dollars Each Year."

☑ Always ask if a seller will hold the financing

Some people are embarrassed to ask about seller financing. They think it gives the impression that they can't borrow money from a traditional lender. Quite the contrary—it shows that you are a knowledgeable and prudent buyer. A surprising number of home owners have no mortgage on their property, and no need to use sale proceeds to buy another home. If they received cash from you, they would have to invest the money somewhere, usually at relatively low interest rates. They might be delighted to be your banker, earning a higher interest rate than they could otherwise obtain. At the same time, you pay a lower interest rate than you could get in the marketplace. If you do obtain seller financing, pay close attention to the checklist in Chapter 20, "Seller Financing." All the terms of the seller financing should be negotiated at the same time as the sale contract—not afterwards.

How it works in the real world: Seller Financing

Courts will not enforce contracts unless they can determine what the parties intended. Important terms must be spelled out. Details and boilerplate can be filled in by a court. Almost all contracts related to real estate—including financing—must be in writing to be enforceable. As a result, any negotiations about seller financing should be included in your real estate purchase contract. Otherwise, the seller could legally change his or her mind about being your lender. Important terms include amount financed, interest rate, term (such as thirty years), and frequency of payments (such as monthly).

Chapter 4:
Shopping for Insurance

Most people wait until the last minute to order their insurance binder for a new home. It's a better idea to start the process sooner, though, because you can learn a lot from insurance agents. They can give you tips about types and locations of homes to buy, which could save you hundreds of dollars a year in insurance premiums. In addition, your credit score and insurance rating affect your premiums. If there are any mistakes in those records, they might need cleaning up, even if they don't affect your loan eligibility.

- ☑ Obtain your C.L.U.E.® score and report
- ☑ Learn what influences your insurance premiums
- ☑ Choose several reputable companies for quotes
- ☑ Compare premiums and deductibles
- ☑ Compare coverages

☑ Obtain your C.L.U.E.® score and report

Most insurance companies obtain outside information to help them evaluate your risk as a potential customer. ChoicePoint is the major provider of this data, called a C.L.U.E.® report (short for Comprehensive Loss Underwriting Exchange).

If you have a history of multiple insurance claims, insurance companies might think you are more likely to make a claim against them if they write insurance for you. It's unfair, but many also believe people with low credit scores are more accident-prone. Be aware that there may be mistakes in your claim history, such as showing that a loss was your fault when it really wasn't. Just like credit scores, this is an area that bears close scrutiny when you are shopping for a home. Your premiums might be higher, or you might even be practically uninsurable, depending on your score.

To order your personal C.L.U.E.® score, you can go online to **www.choicetrust.com**, then click on "C.L.U.E. Reports." You can also call 866-312-8076 and speak with a representative. By law, you must be provided with one free personal report per year. However, you will have to pay for the score.

☑ Learn what influences your insurance premiums

Your C.L.U.E.® score is important, but so are details about the property you want to buy. For example, the term *redlining* comes from drawing red lines around certain areas on a map, and then refusing to make loans or write insurance for people in the area. It used to be very common, was highly discriminatory, and is now illegal if based on race, sex, creed, national origin, or marital status. On the other hand, if insurance companies can demonstrate a legitimate business purpose for redlining certain areas, they may do so. The result could be that some properties cannot obtain insurance, or the premiums may be so high that they place insurance out of reach. (There is a great deal of litigation against insurance companies on this point, as well as on what's outright discrimination and what is secret discrimination disguising itself as "business purpose.") Some states passed consumer protection laws to limit the practice, or at least permit full disclosure of redlined neighborhoods and the reasons for redlining. You'll want to inquire about this when you interview agents or online insurance companies. For more information, call your state's Commissioner of Insurance (or similar department) and ask for the consumer help desk. You can follow the link to your state from the Web page of the National Association of Insurance Commissioners at **www.naic.org/state_web_map.htm**, or call 816-842-3600 for directory assistance.

In addition to location of neighborhoods, specific property factors can affect your premium. Knowing this in advance can help you make more intelligent choices when shopping for a home. The age of the dwelling is important, as is the siding—wood or brick, for example. A brick home is less likely to suffer catastrophic fire damage. Many insurance companies offer significant discounts for monitored fire and security systems. They don't have to be elaborate. Some critical measurements include distance to the nearest fire department, type of fire protection district (volunteer vs. full-time) that would respond to a fire at your property, and distance to the nearest fire hydrant. High crime areas will result in higher premiums.

Flood insurance can be fairly expensive. If the property you are considering buying is in a flood plain, you may want to look for another property or see if the property can be reclassified. Don't forget about flood insurance when shopping. Flood maps do change from time to time. If you're in a flood plain, you can obtain something called an *Elevation Certificate* from a licensed engineer if the property qualifies. It will explain that your property is above the flood level and exempt from lenders' mandatory flood insurance requirements. Be careful, though—most homeowners' policies don't cover flood damage. You might be better off buying flood insurance rather than splitting hairs about whether your property is exempt or not. Flood plain maps are available online at FEMA's website at **www.msc.fema.gov**. Many communities maintain hard copies at their local United States Corps of Engineers, USDA, or HUD offices, where you can view them and obtain assistance interpreting the data.

☑ Choose several reputable companies for quotes

The A.M. Best Company has a rating system for insurance companies. To gain access, go online to **www.ambest.com** and complete the free registration process, or call 908-439-2200 and then press 5742 for customer service to speak to someone who will supply you with ratings. Ratings will give you an idea of the financial strength of an insurance company, and whether it will have enough money to pay large numbers of claims in the event of a catastrophe.

Having enough cash is one thing; being willing to write checks to customers is a completely different issue—one not covered by A.M. Best. Visit **www.badfaithinsurance.org** for information about the worst offenders, the best insurers, and everyone in-between when it comes to paying claims. There's no telephone support for the organization. Non-Internet users should contact their state's Commissioner of Insurance for similar information. Don't forget to ask your friends and current insurance agent or company for advice about customer service and response time for claims.

Once you've selected three or four insurance companies, make sure you ask them for quotes on identical coverages. If you currently have automobile insurance, you may be eligible for a discount if you buy a homeowner's policy from the same company. Be sure to ask insurance companies what your premiums would be if all your insurance needs were placed with the same company.

☑ Compare premiums and deductibles

As a practical matter, most mortgage lenders require you to pay the annual insurance premium up front, and then they collect money each month to keep in an escrow account for the next year's bill. Sometimes, though, a lender will leave insurance payment up to you, personally. When comparing premiums, ask about the rates for annual payments, quarterly payments, and monthly payments. You will find that some companies charge significantly higher rates if you pay premiums in installments.

Mortgage lenders require you to name them as *additional insureds* on policies. That way, they receive notice of default at the same time you do. They are also exempt from some defenses the insurance company might have against you when it comes time to pay a claim. This increases the risk slightly for the insurance company. Some charge a separate fee to add the mortgage lender to the policy. Inquire about this point when obtaining quotes.

You should specify the deductible you want when obtaining quotes. The higher the deductible, the cheaper the premium. If you choose a high deductible, make sure you can afford it if there's a loss. Also remember that an active claim history will result in higher insurance premiums down the road. There's no point in paying the high premiums for a $500 deductible if you won't make any claims less than $1,000 for fear of raising your rates.

☑ Compare coverages

The devil is in the details, as they say. If there's a catastrophic loss, will the insurance company pay fair market value or replacement cost? Just like cars, once your personal possessions leave the store, they're worth a lot less.

Most insurance companies automatically cover personal property up to a certain percentage of the value of the home. If you need more, request more. Pay particular attention to limitations for things like artwork, silver, firearms, furs, jewelry, and collections. If in doubt about what a collection is, ask questions. It's different with different companies.

Make sure living expenses and storage fees during repair or rebuilding are covered. Also ask if there are any maximums for that coverage.

When shopping for insurance, most people only think about what would be covered if something should happen to the property. What could be even more important is the liability coverage offered should someone get injured while on your property. Ask how much liability coverage you automatically get to protect you if someone is injured on your property. It's pretty inexpensive to increase the liability limits, and could be invaluable. Many companies also offer *umbrella policies* for really cheap rates. These pick up where your homeowner's and auto liability policies leave off, and can increase liability limits to several million dollars at a cost of a few hundred dollars a year.

Finally, don't be bashful. Ask each of the three or four insurance companies you select to compare their policies and benefits to the competition's. Don't compare just the prices. If shopping online, look for a customer service number and speak to a live human being about this issue. The education could save you hundreds of dollars and a lot of grief down the road.

Section II:
Shopping

Chapter 5:

Deciding What Features You Want in a Home

Your shopping will be much easier if you decide early what things you must have, what things you detest, and the vast wish list in between those two. At this point, you want enough information to instruct a real estate agent or create an Internet search. You also need to recognize *sudden death* properties—those with any feature that kills the deal and on which you shouldn't waste your time. The final purpose of this exercise is for you to educate yourself about what things to notice when you tour a home. Unless you identify important wish list items ahead of time, you won't think to make a note about them when you visit a home. Some important features include the following.

- ☑ Location
- ☑ Price range
- ☑ Architectural style and age
- ☑ Property amenities
- ☑ Resale value
- ☑ What to do with your list of features

☑ Location

When it comes to location, most people think of school systems first. This is good. Even if you don't have school-age children, the quality of the local schools will affect your resale value in the future.

Looking beyond schools, there are many other location considerations. How long are you willing to spend commuting to work? A deceptively short distance might have massive rush-hour delays, so you'll need to check that out at the appropriate times.

Make a list of the type of businesses you visit once a week or more. You want to make sure similar ones will be near your new home.

Do you require high-speed Internet access, cable television, or city services such as water, sewer, and trash pickup? Is natural gas availability a requirement for gourmet cooking or gas-log fireplaces? For those in sunny climates, do you want the brutal afternoon sun shining in the front or back of your home? If you own a boat or RV (or hope to), or operate a home-based business, neighborhood restrictions against those things will be important to you.

Make a list of all the location considerations that are important to you, and be sure to ask about them when calling for information about properties. You shouldn't waste time touring a home that will never work out because it's in the wrong location.

Here are some ideas to get you started:
- ☑ School zones
- ☑ Voting districts
- ☑ Fire department
- ☑ Public transportation
- ☑ High-speed Internet
- ☑ Utilities
- ☑ Subdivision or not

☑ Existence of sidewalks
☑ Neighborhood parks, playground, pool
☑ Distance to:
  • Work
  • Worship
  • Family
  • Day care
  • Health care
  • Recreation
  • Walk to school
  • Highway access
  • Shopping

☑ Price range

You've already done the calculations for how much home you can afford. It's just a rough estimate, though. Don't let that stop you from inquiring about more expensive homes, or even slightly more economical homes. Many anxious sellers are willing to take substantially less than their asking price. I once offered $150,000 for a home that was listed for $359,000, and the seller accepted! Make sure you factor in upkeep expenses if you buy a larger home than you originally thought you could afford. The utilities and repairs will be higher. You may not be able to keep the house clean without help, and you may need lawn care assistance for an estate-sized lot.

On the other side of the coin, you can find bargains with asking prices below your price range. It doesn't necessarily mean there's anything wrong with the property, but you should be extra cautious when looking at deep discounts. The point is, shop a little bit outside your price range, but don't spend a lot of time or energy at the extremes.

☑ Architectural style and age

Especially if working with a real estate professional, you'll need to be very clear about your likes and dislikes when it comes to the architectural style and age of the property. Don't be vague or polite if you can't stand ranch-style brick homes from the 70s and will never buy one. Just say so!

Some people prefer new homes, because of the freshness and the home builder warranties. Others like homes five to ten years old, because most of the little problems have been fixed and none of the larger systems have started wearing out. Many restrict themselves to historic or older homes, although this is not a good idea for most first-time home buyers.

The maintenance time and expense for an older home is usually an incredible drain, no matter how perfect things look when you first buy. Historic neighborhoods often have strict architectural and landscaping review requirements that could be burdensome to you. If shopping for such a property, make sure you obtain a thorough education regarding all restrictions. I know of one property owner who was required to replace crumbling foundation piers with ones made of the same antique brick as the originals, even though they couldn't be seen from the street! It was horribly time-consuming and expensive.

Is low-maintenance brick, stone, or vinyl siding for you, or do you crave the ability to use new paint colors on the wood every few years? How many floors do you want in your home, and will it make a difference if you plan on owning it when you (and your knees) are older and more worn out? Examine how you live and entertain, and the space needs of any hobbies, and plan accordingly.

☑ Property amenities

Property amenity considerations include the home itself, the land it sits on, and the neighborhood. Most people think about number of bathrooms and bedrooms first. You may need to specify a size for certain rooms, such as something necessary for a large dining room suite. Determine which of the following things are vitally important to you.

- ☑ Large kitchen
- ☑ Formal living room
- ☑ Access for a disability
- ☑ Windows that can be opened for fresh air
- ☑ Attic or basement storage space
- ☑ Enclosed garage
- ☑ Paved road frontage
- ☑ Energy saving devices
- ☑ Manicured lawn
- ☑ Swimming pool
- ☑ Neighborhood park or playground
- ☑ Other:

The possibilities are endless. The important thing is to think about your particular requirements and then shop with them in mind.

For more ideas about the types of things to consider, read Chapter 8, "Comparing Homes." That chapter is really about helping you choose among homes that have some, but not all, of your wants and desires. The lists will help prompt you with ideas for deciding what features you want to begin with.

☑ Resale value

Not everyone needs to worry about resale value. Some people truly will buy a home to live in for their lifetime, or at least a large chunk of it. Most of the rest need to plan ahead to an eventual sale, or should allow for the unforeseen event that they might have to sell in the near future.

If you buy in an area of rapid growth and construction, it may be difficult to recoup your purchase price and closing expenses if you must sell in a year or two, unless prices are climbing dramatically. Why would someone buy your used home when he or she can buy a new one for the same money or only slightly more?

The most expensive home in a neighborhood will usually sell more slowly than an average-priced home. Features that appeal to you as quirky or individualistic will turn off a lot of buyers. The bottom line is, if you anticipate being transferred or buying another home in a year or so, think average, average, average when shopping for a home. The odds will be better for you when it comes time to sell. Don't forget—properties in areas with the best schools will sell the fastest.

☑ What to do with your list of features

Once you have put together your list of features, you need to put them to work. First, organize your lists. One list should contain all the things you *must have* in a home. The *sudden death* list should have all the things you cannot tolerate. The *wish list* should have all the things that would be nice, if available and reasonably priced. This will probably change as you visit homes and discover new things to wish for.

As you shop and speak to owners or real estate agents, ask them all *must have* and *sudden death* questions first. If you don't get the right answers, stop right there. Tell owners your reasons and that you don't want to waste their time or get their hopes up when it won't work out.

Insider trick: Other Properties

If a property doesn't fit your needs, seasoned real estate professionals will ask about the details of your particular requirements. They may have another home that would be perfect. Less experienced agents will not ask you any questions, so you'll need to take up the slack. Inquire if they have anything else that might be right for you.

Finally, don't negotiate with yourself afterwards. If you said you must have sidewalks in the neighborhood, don't try to convince yourself that a bargain price can overcome problems caused by pets and children walking in the streets. Use your lists to shop wisely, and you'll be very pleased with the results.

Chapter 6:
Selecting a
Real Estate Agent

Buying a home is one of the most important decisions you will ever make. It's important to have the best person assisting you, and to have a clear understanding of duties, responsibilities, and compensation.

- ☑ **Understand the different real estate professionals**
- ☑ **Learn about particular specialties**
- ☑ **Determine what you want an agent to do**
- ☑ **Interview several people**
- ☑ **Sign a written contract with clear responsibilities**

☑ Understand the different real estate professionals

In most states, a real estate *broker* is the person legally authorized to enter into contracts to represent consumers in real estate matters. Typically, a *salesperson*, commonly called a *real estate agent*, works under the broker's supervision and authority. In small offices, the broker sometimes also acts as a salesperson, dealing directly with the public. In larger offices, the broker manages the agents, but does not compete with them in trying to earn commissions for him- or herself. Rarely is it important to understand this distinction, so in this book everyone is referred to as agents.

How it works in the real world: Commissions

Most real estate commissions are split four ways. The *listing broker*—the office that signed up the seller—typically receives half of the total commission. He or she must then pay a certain percentage to the agent who actually did all the work. The ratio varies greatly among offices. The *selling broker*—the office that found the buyer—receives the other half of the commission. The selling broker must then pay a percentage to the agent who actually did all the work. This is how everyone makes a living. You might think a commission would be large enough to justify getting more personalized service from an agent, but the agent's split might be so small that he or she can't afford to spend more time with you. That's why it's always best to be organized and efficient, know what you want, and not waste any of the agent's time sightseeing.

A person who takes a listing on a property is a seller's agent. Agents owe very high duties of care, confidentiality, and hard work to their clients. Other real estate professionals from other companies can attempt to sell the same property. That other person might be a subagent, also representing the seller, even though he or she spends all of his or her time with buyers. Subagents owe duties to the seller, also. The agent might be a true buyer's agent, who owes loyalty and allegiance to you, even though he or she is paid by the seller's agent. Agents owe duties to their clients. Everyone else is simply a customer and is owed honesty, but that's all.

Often, you'll have to ask an agent who his or her client is. Unfortunately, many won't even understand the question. If someone says you, the buyer, are his or her client, have it put in writing. It could be important later. Think about this distinction—if you were wrongfully accused of a crime, would you hire a lawyer who referred to you as a client, or one who referred to you as a customer? It's an entirely different feel, isn't it? That's because everyone knows, intuitively, the difference in responsibilities to customers and clients.

In real estate, because of history and customs in an area, your only choice as a buyer might be to work as someone's customer. Don't let that discourage you, but take all advice and information with a grain of salt, and don't reveal anything confidential.

How it works in the real world: Client Confidentiality

There are bad apples in every bunch, and the real estate profession is no exception. Sellers' agents are supposed to keep their client's confidences, and to obtain the highest purchase price possible. Many agents will show you houses listed by someone else, but they will be operating as the seller's subagent rather than as your agent. If that person tells you something similar to, "The owner is asking $200,000, but I know she'll take a lot less because she's an inch away from bankruptcy," then he or she is violating his or her ethical responsibilities. Beware! Someone ignorant of ethics requirements is a loose cannon— you could be the next one to get hurt.

Rarely, you might work with a *transaction broker* or in another type of limited obligation relationship. Such people must keep the confidentiality of any private information you reveal to them, but they owe no particular negotiating or advisory responsibilities to either side. Some states allow brokers to represent buyers and sellers at the same time on the same piece of real estate, but it's hard to understand how this can work in the real world. The parties have competing interests, after all!

It's best to hire a buyer's agent, but there might be drawbacks. Depending on your contract, you might owe a fee if the agent finds exactly what you said you were looking for, and you then decide not to buy for some reason. Ask a few real estate brokers and mortgage lenders about what's typical in your community. See if the title or escrow companies can provide advice and recommendations. They usually know who does a good job, and who always seems to have problems at the closing table.

☑ Learn about particular specialties

Most experienced agents specialize in a particular price range, part of town, or type of housing, such as historic homes, new construction, or raw land. It allows them to operate more efficiently. Newer agents tend to work with anyone who wanders through the door. They're less likely to be as knowledgeable as the specialists, but they're also less likely to write you off if they sense you're a picky customer who will take up a lot of time looking at large numbers of properties. Decide which attributes you want and choose accordingly.

Even if you go with a *general practitioner* type of broker, do take the time to find out the names of agents who specialize in the types of properties you might want. Open houses conducted by sellers' agents will be invaluable in helping you refine your opinions and improve your shopping skills.

How it works in the real world: Open Houses

Listing agents hold open houses for three reasons. First, it makes the seller feel like some work is going on. Sellers don't know that, except for new subdivisions under construction, open houses rarely generate buyers for that particular property. Second, all the nosy neighbors can satisfy their curiosity without wasting the agent's time pretending to be prospects. Third, lots of shoppers fill out the guest book and the agent can contact them about other properties, even if the current one isn't quite right. That's right—open houses sell lots of *other* real estate on which agents have listings! So, don't be bashful about visiting as many as possible in order to educate yourself. Be honest about your timeline and financial considerations. You won't offend the agent.

☑ Determine what you want an agent to do

Some people want an agent who's almost an employee. Such buyers want to assign very specific tasks, such as obtaining certain details about particular properties. Others want an advisor to assist in refining the search process, look for properties meeting the buyer's needs, and provide a great deal of generalized insight about schools, neighborhoods, resale values, and so on. Make sure you understand what you want your agent to do for you and communicate it clearly to the agent. A highly nurturing person will be offended if you are abrupt and want answers to direct questions and nothing more. A "just the facts, ma'am" type agent won't volunteer anything, and might cause you to feel neglected and uninformed.

☑ Interview several people

Nice real estate agents get lots of referrals. It doesn't mean they are the most competent to do the job, it might just mean they have the widest circle of acquaintances and haven't alienated any of them. After you find two or three agents you think are qualified, take the time to speak with them in person. You should ask each one the following questions.

- ☑ How long have you lived in this community and how do you keep up with housing trends and values?
- ☑ What kinds of property do you specialize in? If you don't specialize in my kind, what expertise do you have to help me anyway?
- ☑ Do you work primarily within a certain price range or area? Can you describe this to me? (Note: An agent who spends most of his or her time with $300,000+ properties south of town will not be the best choice for something north of town in the $175,000 price range.)

☑ How long does it usually take you to find a home for some-one? What happens if I take four times longer than the average?

☑ Do you have any materials I can use to help educate me about house hunting?

☑ How many closings have you had in the past year? For what percentage were you the selling agent?

☑ What system do you have to remind you about my wants if a suitable house becomes available six months from now? Would you contact me?

Ask each one if he or she will act as your agent, or as the subagent for various sellers. There's nothing wrong with being a subagent, but make sure you don't reveal any confidential information to one, such as the highest amount you can afford to spend. If you work with a subagent who represents sellers, then you can work with several of them simultaneously. Just keep track of who shows you which properties, so the right person will be paid when you buy.

In your interviews, pay attention to the ebb and flow of the conversations. Do the agents listen to you and answer your questions, or do they spend all their time talking and selling themselves? Are they willing to give you advice or waiting until you sign on the dotted line? How much experience do these agents have? If new to the business, are they willing to work extra hard to earn your respect? How are they compensated—by the seller or by you? In their opinion, how long does it take someone with your needs to find a home at a reasonable price? How organized do they seem to be? Here's a trick—walk the person to his or her car when you leave. If it's a mess, that's a good sign he or she lacks personal pride or professionalism. You're placing a lot of trust in this person. You need to be comfortable that he or she can deliver what he or she promises.

☑ Sign a written contract with clear responsibilities

Buyers' agents, who legally represent you, will have a form contract for you to sign. Make sure you read it thoroughly and ask for explanations for anything you don't understand. Remember, just because it's a form doesn't mean it's not negotiable. If you are unhappy with any terms, speak up and try to get them changed. Pay particular attention to any clauses having to do with payment. You might be liable for a fee even if you buy nothing. If you are in doubt on this point, ask about it and write the answer at the bottom of the contract.

Sellers' subagents usually don't have any written contracts for buyers, but it's a good idea to have a letter or something that spells out your expectations. Does he or she prefer phone or email communications? Will the agent show you properties listed by other brokers? How often will he or she return your phone calls if you want him or her to check on something? Will he or she let you know about open houses for properties meeting your requirements? Can he or she give you seller disclosure reports before you make an offer, or only afterwards? Add anything else the agent told you he or she could do for you—these things are usually viewed by the agent as *sales hype* until someone writes them down and requires a signature.

Chapter 7:

Shopping For Sale By Owner (FSBO) Properties

If you are working with a real estate agent, they usually will not tell you about the For Sale By Owner (FSBO) market. That's because the seller will probably not pay a commission, so there's no way for the agent to make any money. You'll need to shop for such properties on your own. Some buyers prefer to concentrate on FSBOs (pronounced fizz-bose), believing the prices will be lower. This is not always true. The following are some guidelines to assist you in your search.

- ☑ **Prepare a questionnaire**
- ☑ **Learn about school zones**
- ☑ **Identify sources for FSBO information**
- ☑ **Research property values**
- ☑ **Make the most of your appointments**
- ☑ **Be ready to write your own contract and perform all follow-up**

☑ Prepare a questionnaire

For some reason, most people don't mind calling a real estate agent several times as they think of new questions. They're reluctant to do the same thing with a FSBO, though. It's complicated by the fact that you tend to get into conversations with home sellers, discussing all the different things you have in common. You form a relationship, and then forget to ask many important questions. In order to avoid this problem, create a list of all the questions you'd like to ask about any property—size of house and lot; restrictive covenants; recent repairs; school zones; utilities; age of house, roof, and HVAC; and, anything else you can think of. Start out with the *must have* and the *sudden death* features you identified in Chapter 5. Don't forget to ask the price, and whether there's any flexibility.

Write down the address, the owner's name, and the date of your phone call at the top of the questionnaire. Make price the very first thing on your list, in case the property is way outside your price range. Also, make it the last question. The owner may feel defensive after answering all your other questions, and might indicate a willingness to take less money.

☑ Learn about school zones

School zones are such an important selling feature that almost all homeowners know their schools, even if they don't have young children. Knowing that Roberts Elementary is on the east side of town, but you want to live on the west side, will save you a lot of time and trouble if you discover this early. Armed with the knowledge that Mountain Brook High School is the best in the city and Roberts Valley is the worst, you can sift through properties fairly efficiently. These things will also affect your own resale values down the road, so it's an important consideration, whether you have children or not.

☑ Identify sources for FSBO information

The best source—although not the easiest—is to ride around the neighborhoods, looking for "for sale" signs. Usually they're the kind available from an office supply store, with a space for a handwritten telephone number. If the home has been on the market for any length of time, the phone number may be faded and hard to read from a car. Most people will not stop, get out, and try to decipher the sign. Such signs are good indicators of motivated sellers who are getting desperate because they aren't receiving any calls, since their sign is so faded no one can read the numbers.

Read the classified ads of your local newspapers every day. Popular wisdom says new ads do best on Wednesdays and Sundays. Many sellers don't know that, though, and could start theirs on some other day. In a tight market, one day could make a difference in buying your dream home or not. Don't forget about local classified magazines, such as *Penny Thrift* or *Neighborhood Shopper*. They usually print only once a week and are poorly organized, but the advertising rates are cheap and many sellers use them. Finally, grocery store and church bulletin boards are a good source of flyers about homes for sale.

Insider trick: Let Sellers Find You

People thinking about selling their homes usually scan the classifieds regularly in order to develop an idea of the value of their home. Run a small ad under the title "Wanted to Buy," with your basic needs and contact information. Do the same thing if you find a community bulletin board with lots of "For Sale" flyers on it. Divorce lawyers, bankruptcy lawyers, and ministers often know about motivated sellers and may be willing to refer people to you. You might obtain a call from someone who hasn't even put his or her home on the market yet. It's a great opportunity to purchase something without any pressure from other potential buyers.

There are many online FSBO services where buyers can list their properties. You can do an Internet search on "FSBO," and your city and state. Check out all the relevant Web pages—there's no dominant player in this market yet.

☑ Research property values

Just because an owner is asking a certain price doesn't mean it's what the property is worth or that the owner wouldn't take less money. Many sellers price their homes according to what they need to get rather than what they're actually worth.

Once you develop an interest in a particular property or neighborhood, find out what other homes are selling for in the area. Real estate company advertisements in home sale magazines or Sunday newspaper supplements will give you an idea of asking prices. Lenders or mortgage brokers usually have a good feel for actual selling prices, and might be willing to advise you. If you're aware of recent sales in the area, you can usually visit the local tax assessor's office, provide the addresses, and find out the sale prices. Sometimes this information is available online.

☑ Make the most of your appointments

Real estate agents usually have brochures or online Web pages with photos and other information about their listed properties. It's easy for you to refresh your memory after several viewings start to run together in your mind. You can't do the same thing with a FSBO.

When you schedule your appointment for a tour, take several things with you. Using a digital camera, make your first photo a sheet of paper with the property address and the owner's name. That will help keep straight what photos go with which properties—the photo of the paper acts like a movie credit, telling you what comes next. Take a picture of the front of the house, the two neighboring properties, and the one across the street. Always do them in the same order, such as left house, then right house, then across the street house. That way, you won't get confused later. Make as many photos as possible of anything else.

Take a tape recorder with you and make a running commentary as you view the property. An example would be, "I'm in the kitchen, which has a six-burner, gas cooktop; stainless steel appliances; a counter separating it from the family room; and, a large picture window looking into the backyard and the pool." You would never write down all this information, but it may be important to you later. Keep track the easy way—with a tape recorder. Use a separate tape for each property. Tape is cheap.

Insider trick: Things to Take to an Appointment
- ☑ Graph paper for sketching
- ☑ Hand-held tape recorder with extra batteries and tape
- ☑ Digital camera
- ☑ Notepad (some thoughts can't be recorded because you don't want the seller to overhear them)
- ☑ Tape measure at least 20´ long
- ☑ List of questions you want to ask the seller

After you've completed the tour, spend time getting to know the owner. You don't want to do this first, because the process of creating a relationship will keep you from asking many important questions. However, it is important to get a sense of the seller, his or her motivation for selling (and price flexibility), and any discomfort he or she might have about particular features or potential problems. Let the seller do most of the talking. Say "I see" or "that's interesting" several times, with long pauses afterwards. This usually makes people nervous and they talk in order to fill the quiet spaces. In the process, they reveal more information than they intended.

Insider trick: Questions to Ask

☑ Do you have a survey/appraisal/home inspection report (any or all of them)?

☑ How old are the roof/appliances/HVAC/water heater/carpet/ house?

☑ Is anything still under warranty?

☑ Can you supply me with a list of the utility bill amounts for the past year?

☑ Do you have a termite bond?

☑ What appliances/window treatments/light fixtures stay with the home after the sale?

☑ How much is insurance/real estate taxes/association dues?

☑ What has been repaired or updated within the past year?

☑ Do the roof/basement/walls/chimney/windows/pipes/toilets/ faucets leak?

☑ How often do the circuit breakers pop?

☑ When was the fireplace/septic tank/HVAC ductwork last cleaned?

☑ Are there any disputes regarding property lines/association rules/pets/noisy neighbors?

☑ When was the last time the police came to the neighborhood? Why?

☑ Would you take less money or hold the financing?

If any questions seem to invite a follow-up question, go for it. Don't be content to ask how often the circuit breakers pop. If it's often, ask why.

If you have any potential interest in the property, give your name and phone number to the seller. Who knows—you might lose the phone number, or he or she might call you out of the clear blue sky and offer a deep discount. It never hurts to make yourself easy to reach.

☑ Be ready to write your own contract and perform all follow-up

If you found the perfect home at a terrific price and the seller was willing to hold the financing at 1% below market rates and $0 down, would you be ready to act quickly, before someone else stole it out from under you? You need to have the following items on hand at all times.

☑ Written offer with blanks for important negotiated terms
☑ Written seller financing agreement with amount to be financed, term, and interest rate
☑ Blank seller disclosure form, if one is required in your state
☑ Escrow agreement for someone to hold the earnest money

Real estate contracts vary from state to state, depending on local customs and laws. You can usually download one from the Internet or obtain a sample from a real estate office, mortgage broker, or local (not a chain) office supply store. A good site is **www.uslegalforms.com** (or you can call them at 877-389-0141).

Ask a real estate attorney to spend an hour with you explaining the various terms of your contract forms and why they are or are not important. This will cost you a couple hundred dollars, but it will be money well spent. Tape-record the conversation, because you won't be able to take notes rapidly enough. Any real estate attorney worth a darn can translate a form real estate contract in an hour or less. Armed with the explanations, you'll know which clauses are really important, which ones are negotiable, and which ones might work against you and should be deleted.

Make absolutely certain your contract includes contingency clauses so you can cancel it if your financing falls through, the property fails its inspection, there are boundary line discrepancies, you can't get a building permit if you need one, or the seller can't deliver good and clear title. Chapter 17 addresses the mechanics of writing offers.

If the seller will hold financing, you want a written seller financing agreement at first, rather than a full-blown note and mortgage. That's because a seller presented with a note and mortgage will usually panic a little bit and require time to speak to his or her advisors. These are long, scary, documents that require scrutiny. A one-page document can say the following.

"Seller agrees to hold the financing in the amount of $_____ at _____% interest, payable in equal monthly installments over the course of _____ years, with the first payment due 30 days after closing, and Buyer agrees that this is an important consideration in Buyer's agreement to purchase the property."

The one-page document seems innocent enough; all parties sign and it's legally binding. The next day, give the seller the full note and mortgage for review.

Check with your state's real estate commission to see if sellers must provide a disclosure statement to buyers. Ideally, you'd like to get one before you make an offer. Sometimes sellers aren't required to give one until after they receive a written offer, but the contract can be cancelled if the disclosures are unacceptable. Find out how this works in your area.

Never let the seller hold the earnest money, even (perhaps especially) if it's a friend or relative. It's not an issue of honesty, but of having a disinterested stranger in charge of the funds.

You'll need a written escrow agreement naming a person or company who has agreed to hold the money and disburse it according to instructions. Usually, this will be the closing company or title company. Some charge a separate fee, some do not.

How it works in the real world: Earnest Money Basics

Make sure your contract has only two choices regarding the disposition of the earnest money:

1. all parties agree in writing before the money is paid to anyone OR
2. a court, or arbitrator, will decide who gets the money, with the loser to pay all costs and fees.

If there's no real estate agent involved, you'll need to make sure everything is completed on time for the closing. (see Chapter 23, "Information to Give the Title or Escrow Company.") Remember, you're not just buying a home—you're managing a closing process. You and the seller are the only people motivated to make sure everything happens on time. All other parties—the title company, the lender, any inspectors or appraisers—will all assume your business is in the bag, and they will have a tendency to move on to generating other new business. Delays will not affect them. Delays could be deadly to you if you don't close on time and the seller can cancel the contract as a result, or if you lose an attractive interest rate. Examine your strengths and weaknesses honestly. If managing this process is not going to work, hire someone to do it, such as a lawyer or financial advisor.

Chapter 8:
Comparing Homes

Some real estate agents like to show houses early in the day, when you're fresh, eager, and impressionable. Others prefer to show houses late in the day after you've seen five or six others. They hope you're tired and can't remember what property has which features, and so will better remember the last one you see. Both extremes rely on faulty memory for their strategies. Don't get caught in that trap. Create an easy-to-use system for comparing properties and revisiting their pros and cons long after your walk-through.

- ☑ **Determine what method of keeping track of information works for you**
- ☑ **Decide what information is important**
- ☑ **Read Chapter 14, "Comparing Land for Construction"**
- ☑ **Invest in a digital or disposable camera**

☑ Determine what method of keeping track of information works for you

I put everything on my computer—my whole life is there. It's easy and it works for me. For you, think about how you keep track of information and go with it. Maybe it's a refrigerator covered with yellow stickie notes, file folders in a cabinet, stacks of shoe boxes crammed with paper, or handwritten comments in the margins of home buyer magazines. Pick something, and then stick with it for your house hunting. The bottom line is, make sure all information about a particular home is kept together and can be retrieved easily.

☑ Decide what information is important

This is going to be different from the list in Chapter 5, "Deciding What Features You Want in a Home." Your *must have* and your *sudden death* items probably won't change over time. However, as you become a more educated shopper, you'll find your list of important features getting longer. With house #1, you might not think to ask if high-speed Internet is available. After hearing homeowner #6 brag about his or her DSL service, you might not take this for granted any more. Don't worry— just add this to the list. If house #1 is still in the running at the end, make another phone call or schedule another visit to inquire about all the additional items.

The following lists provide some ideas about things that might be important to you. Before you read any further, write down your own thoughts. Otherwise, your head will be filled with these topics and you'll forget some of your own.

☑ Location:

- ☑ voting districts
- ☑ school zones
- ☑ nearby zoning
- ☑ drive time to work (time this during rush hour and don't just measure the distance)
- ☑ proximity to religious facilities
- ☑ day care
- ☑ shopping
- ☑ health care
- ☑ recreation
- ☑ dining
- ☑ public transportation (even if you don't use public transportation, it may be important to household helpers)
- ☑ urban, suburban, *exurban* (typically prosperous semi-rural communities past the suburbs and clustered around major feeder routes into the cities), or truly rural setting

☑ Construction:

- ☑ age of home
- ☑ type of siding
- ☑ type of roofing
- ☑ built on slab, crawl space, or basement construction

☑ Floorplan:

- ☑ number of bedrooms
- ☑ number of bathrooms
- ☑ number of half-baths
- ☑ bedrooms with private baths
- ☑ minimum size of bedrooms
- ☑ formal dining and living rooms
- ☑ open kitchen and family area, or separate
- ☑ one level or two
- ☑ master bedroom on which floor

☑ wide hallways and doors for wheelchair access
☑ in-law or adult child apartment
☑ separate laundry room
☑ attic or basement storage
☑ number and size of closets
☑ porches and decks
☑ garage or carport
☑ how many vehicles accommodated

☑ Features:
☑ central heat and air-conditioning
☑ energy-efficient systems
☑ central vacuum
☑ gourmet kitchen appliances
☑ specific materials used for countertops
☑ cabinets and flooring
☑ security system
☑ intercom or music system
☑ sophisticated telecom pre-wiring
☑ elevator
☑ luxury master bath
☑ ceiling fans
☑ fireplace
☑ fireplace heat recirculators
☑ windows that can be opened
☑ swimming pool or spa
☑ sprinkler system for lawn
☑ gated community
☑ paved roads (don't laugh—many rural homes front on dirt roads)
☑ heated garage in cold climates
☑ golf cart garage for golf course communities

☑ **Yard:**
- ☑ landscaped
- ☑ natural
- ☑ large
- ☑ small
- ☑ trees or grass only
- ☑ sunny places for flowers and vegetables
- ☑ privacy features
- ☑ outdoor lighting
- ☑ outdoor music

☑ **Neighborhood:**
- ☑ active homeowners association or no controls at all
- ☑ sidewalks
- ☑ play areas for children
- ☑ amenities (such as tennis courts)
- ☑ walking trails or swimming pool
- ☑ neighbors with similar interests (read the bumper stickers, check out children's toys, or go to a local garage sale if possible)
- ☑ how well other homes are maintained
- ☑ a preponderance of burglar bars in windows
- ☑ any leash laws or pets roaming free

☑ **Utilities:**
- ☑ natural gas possible
- ☑ LP gas tanks allowed
- ☑ cable television, high-speed Internet access, or fiber-optic telephone cable (*fiber to the curb*) for advanced telecommunications services, such as Internet, long-distance telephone, and downloadable movies

☑ Price:
- ☑ what is the asking price
- ☑ what is the likely sale price
- ☑ how likely will the home hold its value

☑ Other:
- ☑ anything else that occurs to you

Make a master checklist with the most important features at the top, descending to least important. When comparing properties, you might decide that one really memorable, important feature—like a swimming pool—might be less persuasive than a lot of other features and proximity to a neighborhood pool. Without a system for comparing properties, that backyard pool might stick in your mind, crowding out all other considerations and possibly leading you to a poor overall choice.

☑ Read Chapter 14, "Comparing Land for Construction"

If a property has a septic tank system rather than public sewer, be sure to read that section of Chapter 14, "Comparing Land." Likewise, if you plan to build any additions or improvements onto an existing home, many of the considerations important in new construction will be equally relevant to you.

☑ Invest in a digital or disposable camera

After about five homes, you won't be able to remember what any of them look like. (Also, some features might not be noticed or memorable until you see something else, and you'll wonder if an earlier home had a similar amenity.) If you have a digital camera, take as many pictures as you can—it's free. You don't have to print all of them—just be sure you keep them in separate folders on your computer, labeled with the address of the home. Remember this trick from an earlier chapter: make your first photo a piece of paper with the street address of the property and the name of the real estate agent or seller.

If you're using a disposable camera, you probably won't take as many pictures. Be sure to get at least one shot of the curb view of the home, the neighbors on either side, the back yard, any important rooms inside, and the entrance to the community if it's in a subdivision.

Chapter 9:
Comparing Condos

If you haven't already done so, read Chapter 8, "Comparing Homes." Much of the same information will be important to you. However, you do have some additional considerations when shopping for a condominium, including the following.

- ☑ Consider the age of the project
- ☑ Discover the personality of the community
- ☑ Weigh different restrictions
- ☑ Inventory common area features
- ☑ Calculate monthly dues
- ☑ Evaluate resale value

☑ Consider the age of the project

The age of the project refers to the condominium project itself, not the buildings. Do you want something under construction or undergoing conversion so you can take advantage of early sale discounts and maximum flexibility in choice of units? Or, would you rather things be a little more settled, with no surprises about community personality (see next section) or finances? Many times, condo developers will set monthly dues as low as possible in order to attract buyers. Only later do the homeowners discover the funds are insufficient to make repairs as needed, replace or update landscaping, and cover increased property taxes after the rebates expire. On the other hand, older communities have more maintenance issues than newer ones. If you're buying for the short term, brand-new might be best for you.

☑ Discover the personality of the community

Some condo communities have high numbers of investor-owners and tenant-occupants. Typically, those owners will not vote for rehab projects or even major repairs, because the higher monthly dues will not pay for themselves. In other words, the existence of a swimming pool might allow a landlord to charge only $20 per month more in rent and still be competitive with area apartments. The cost of repairs, plus monthly pool maintenance expenses, might not be worth it to the landlords. You will be outvoted if you want the pool repaired.

Other personality considerations should be whether the projects are child-friendly, family-oriented, elder-conscious, or mainly home to upwardly mobile transient owners. All of these things will impact voting in the community, and will affect your quality of life and your resale value.

☑ Weigh different restrictions

When shopping, be sure to get an overview of the CC&Rs—Covenants, Conditions, and Restrictions—at each community. You'll need to read them in detail before making any offer, but the high points should be sufficient for comparison shopping. Pets might not be allowed. There may be restrictions on the number of nonfamily members residing in the unit. This could be important for people requiring full-time care or live-in housekeepers. Something as minor as a prohibition against signage might be critically important if you are politically active. The condos might forbid leasing, or may make it extremely expensive because of monthly impact fees, background checks on tenants, or other such things. This may not be important today, but what if you are transferred and can't sell your unit? Wouldn't you want the ability to rent it out?

☑ Inventory common area features

What amenities are important to you? Which ones don't add any value to your life? If you don't care about them, might they be important for resale value? Remember, the more recreational and common features a project has, the more expensive the monthly dues will be (unless there is some sort of pay-as-you-use program in place).

How many elevators does the building have, and how long is the wait when you summon one? Do there seem to be adequate fire escapes? Is there sufficient parking for tenants, and does a parking place cost extra?

What electrical loads are allotted for each unit? The building manager should be able to tell you this, or it might be in the CC&Rs. An older building might not accommodate all the power requirements for a home office, media room, gourmet kitchen, and luxury bath. The result could be constant power problems or an individual assessment to improve service. You might need to concentrate on new construction to get an ample electrical allotment.

☑ Calculate monthly dues

A low purchase price might be more than offset by high monthly dues. In addition, you'll need to inquire about upcoming assessments that could affect your buying decision, and whether there is a move afoot to increase dues. These things will need to be factored in when comparing properties.

☑ Evaluate resale value

Resale value is important when buying any property, but it's particularly critical with condos, because of all the buying frenzy in the recent past, driving up prices at incredible rates. If you plan to live in your unit for only a short time, make sure you buy in a stable area that seems to be holding value well. Buyers looking for long-term housing can be more flexible. In the event of any downturn in the market, they can simply remain in their condo and wait out possible price drops until values stabilize again.

NOTE: *For more detailed information about buying condos, and an excellent resource for all phases of shopping, financing, and buying, purchase a copy of "How to Buy a Condominium or Townhouse" (Sourcebooks, 2006) by me—Denise L. Evans.*

Chapter 10:
Buying a Co-Op Apartment

If you're skipping around in this book, go back and read Chapter 8, "Comparing Homes" and Chapter 9, "Comparing Condos." Many of the ideas will be relevant to you when shopping for a cooperative apartment. There are a few additional items you should include in your personal checklists. This is due to the peculiar nature of a co-op. You will not buy real estate. Instead, you will buy stock in a corporation that owns a building. As a shareholder, you will be entitled to rent (yes, rent!) a particular apartment, from which you can be evicted under some circumstances. These factors create the need for a little extra work.

- ☑ **Compare all financial aspects of purchase and ownership**
- ☑ **Determine how difficult it is to obtain Board approval for purchase**
- ☑ **Find out if there is building security and full-time maintenance**
- ☑ **Identify potential lenders early**

☑ Compare all financial aspects of purchase and ownership

When you buy a co-op apartment, you buy stock in a corporation that owns a building. This gives you the right to enter into a *proprietary lease* for a particular unit. You pay monthly rent, but it's usually significantly less than similar traditional apartments. As you shop, you'll need to pay particular attention to five financial areas:

☑ purchase price;

☑ monthly rent;

☑ utilities;

☑ maintenance of your apartment; and,

☑ flip tax on resale—amount you must share with the building.

A low purchase price and resulting low mortgage payments might be counterbalanced by high monthly rent. This brings up an additional question: what does the rent include?

Some co-ops pay all utilities and then cover the expense within the monthly rent. Others have individual utility meters, and you buy your service directly from the power company, phone company, and so on. Still other buildings buy utilities in bulk and then submeter them to the tenants at a profit.

You'll need to find out if the building makes all repairs within the apartments (which would justify a higher rent) or if tenants must obtain board approval for repairs, but pay for them individually. Sometimes, repairs are performed by the building maintenance person, but then billed to individual owners on some sort of time and materials basis.

Usually, some portion of the rent goes to mortgage payments on the building. For older buildings, you'll need to inquire about the remaining years on the mortgage. Will it pay off soon, and if so, will the rent decrease?

Finally, flip tax policies will dramatically affect your financial picture. Many cooperative apartment buildings require the seller to share a portion of his or her sale proceeds with the building. It might be a percentage of the profit, a percentage of the gross sales price, a flat fee, or some complicated formula based on square footage or other such things. Usually, the higher the flip tax, the lower the monthly rent, because the building can cover some of its expenses from flip tax proceeds. Be very careful about flip taxes expressed as a percentage of gross sale proceeds—this could leave you with insufficient money after a sale to pay off your lender.

☑ Determine how difficult it is to obtain Board approval for purchase

Just because the apartment owner wants you to buy his or her unit, and you have the cash on hand, doesn't mean the Board of Directors of the co-op will approve the deal. The courts give great latitude to Boards in this regard, and allow them to disapprove buyers for almost any reason except the legally prohibited ones like sex, race, marital status, and so on.

Most sellers, in an excess of optimism, will tell you it's easy to obtain Board approval. You should ask more searching questions, such as "Who's been turned down for purchase, and why?" or "What was *your* approval process like?" Depending on the answers, rank each co-op project as an "A," "C," or "F" for ease of Board approval, with "A" being the easiest, "C" being about average, and "F" meaning nearly impossible. Depending on your ultimate goals and comfort with your own acceptability to the Board, an "F" co-op might be just the thing for you!

☑ Find out if there is building security and full-time maintenance

Building security and full-time maintenance might be more important in some buildings than others. If you plan to be a short-term owner in a brand-new building next to a police sub-station, you might not want to pay the additional overhead for security and maintenance. For some people, it might be a deal killer for any building that lacks such services. You'll need to be sure to ask about how such services are compensated, including tipping policies and expectations.

☑ Identify potential lenders early

It's more difficult to obtain co-op financing than a loan for a condo or detached housing, because co-ops are merely leases within a building owned by a separate corporation. You buy stock in the building, but have no rights in the real estate. Under some circumstances, you can be evicted, making you much less motivated to make your loan payments. Other times, the master lender might foreclose on the whole building, leaving you—and your bank—with nothing. This makes many lenders nervous—they just aren't set up to deal with the paperwork and the oversight. The following are some lenders that specialize in co-op loans (you may be able to find others).

Apple Bank for Savings
914-902-2775
www.theapplebank.com

Bank of New York Mortgage Company
800-480-8773
www.bnymortgage.com

Bank of America
888-293-0264
www.bankofamerica.com

JPMorgan Chase Mortgage
800-848-9136
www.chase.com/mortgage

CitiBank, FSB
800-374-9700
www.citibank.com

Dime Savings Bank of Williamsburgh
800-321-3463
www.dimedirect.com

Emigrant Mortgage Company
888-364-4726
www.emigrant.com

HSBC Bank USA
800-975-4722
www.hsbc.com

Washington Mutual Savings
800-788-7000
www.wamu.com

In shopping for co-ops, you'll need to keep in mind any restrictions the lenders have regarding particular buildings, higher or lower interest rates for conversions, attractive deals if they also hold the building master mortgage, and other such things. It's not as easy to obtain co-op lending as it is for a condo or detached housing. For that reason, you'll have to compare lender requirements at the same time you compare property amenities—you won't have a lot of lender alternatives.

Chapter 11:

Comparing New Manufactured Housing

Manufactured housing is something built entirely in a factory and then transported to the land where it will be installed. These used to be called mobile homes. *Modular housing* is something different: partially built in a factory, transported to the site, and then assembled for final installation. Because manufactured housing typically targets a low-income market, there are widespread abuses in pricing, warranties, and financing. All manufactured housing must comply with minimum quality standards imposed by the U.S. Department of Housing and Urban Development (HUD), but better homes will exceed those standards. When comparing homes, pay particular attention to the following things.

- ☑ **Know where the home will be installed**
- ☑ **Investigate the manufacturers' history and reputation**
- ☑ **Obtain copies of manufacturer's warranties**
- ☑ **Require unbundled quotes**
- ☑ **Recognize financing risks**

☑ Know where the home will be installed

If you plan to place your home on rented land, you can count on some difficulty obtaining financing, higher closing costs, and a higher interest rate than traditional housing. That's because the moment your home is delivered to the site, it's worth significantly less than you paid for it. The collateral—your home—isn't worth what's owed on it. Lenders don't like that situation, so they charge higher interest rates to cover the additional risk. Don't let that scare you into accepting the dealer's financing package, because that will typically cost you the highest interest rates. Do be prepared to shop for your loan. Some lenders will offer you better rates if you sign at least a five-year lease for your site.

☑ Investigate the manufacturer's history and reputation

Make sure you check out the dealer (the company selling the home) and the manufacturer (the company that built the home). Warranties are worthless if the manufacturer never honors them, or takes advantage of fine print and arbitration clauses to effectively void all of its warranties. An irresponsible dealer can sell you a fine, well-built product, but hurt you in other areas such as the quality and price of appliance upgrades, damage during transportation, or improper installation once on-site.

Start with the Better Business Bureau to find any complaints filed there. Go online to search for blogs or user groups for that manufacturer. The U.S. Department of Housing and Urban Development (HUD) has entered into cooperative agreements with thirty-eight states to inspect plants and respond to consumer complaints. For more information, call HUD at 800-927-2891 or check out their Web page at **www.hud.gov/offices/hsg/sfh/mhs/mhshome.cfm**.

When shopping, be sure to ask for references, including customers who have owned their homes for three to five years. That's the time period when problems will begin appearing if there are construction defects.

Finally, you might want to check courthouse records to see if there have been any lawsuits against the dealer or manufacturer. Both usually have arbitration clauses in their contracts, and arbitration cases are not public records. However, many plaintiffs' lawyers start their lawsuits in the state's trial courts, only to be transferred to arbitration later. At least you will find a lawyer's name and someone to talk to. It's a start.

☑ Obtain copies of manufacturer's warranties

Federal law requires all dealers to maintain copies of the warranties for the homes they sell. They don't have to give you a copy, but they do have to let you read it if you ask. Be a pest if they won't make a copy for you—insist on reading every word, out loud, and ask someone to explain the language to you. You should also ask the following warranty-related questions.

- ☑ What other warranties come with the home, such as dealer, transporter, and installer?
- ☑ What is specifically excluded from the warranties?
- ☑ What will void the warranties?
- ☑ How long do the warranties last?
- ☑ Do the warranties cover parts and labor, just parts, or just labor?
- ☑ Do warranty values reduce over time as the home gets older?
- ☑ Who does the warranty work, and do they come out to the home site?

☑ Require unbundled quotes

Most dealers like to quote you a package price for the manufactured home, upgraded features and appliances, a home full of furniture, transportation and installation, and financing. They'll tell you they can put you in the home in one week for only $632.15 per month. Most people never read the fine print to discover the outrageous prices they pay for all components of the *bundled quote*, the high closing costs, and the high interest rate. They don't realize they'll be paying $632.15 per month practically forever. The only way to compare deals is to require sellers to quote you a price for the home, and then separate prices and rates for everything else. Once the light of day hits all the unbundled pieces, they tend to shrivel up and get smaller!

☑ Recognize financing risks

Financing a manufactured home carries its own unique risks for borrower and lender. They both revolve around the fact that the home depreciates dramatically once it leaves the dealer's lot. It's typical to finance purchases with little or no money down. Often, the closing costs are rolled into the financing, so the buyer doesn't have to bring any money at all to the closing table. The loan is said to be *upside-down*, meaning the collateral (your home) is worth a lot less than the loan balance. To compensate, lenders charge very high interest rates. That way, if you default, they won't get hurt very badly, because they're making so much money off everyone else.

If you can purchase a piece of land on which to place your home, you may be able to finance the two together and obtain a better interest rate. Best of all would be to buy some land and pay cash for it, or obtain land by gift from a family member. By giving the home and the land as collateral, you'll be able to improve your rates.

The flip side of this problem is for the buyer. If you purchase manufactured housing as a short-term solution until
you can afford *site-built housing*, you may be in for an
unpleasant surprise. Your home will be worth substantially
less than the loan balance. That means you'll have to kick in
extra money to pay off the loan when you sell your home. It's
hard enough to come up with the down payment and closing
costs for a new home, much less another $10,000 or so to pay
off the old one. If you think this is going to cause you problems in the future, consider buying a used home that has
already depreciated. Or, delay buying anything and continue
saving money, or buy a smaller site-built home for the time
being.

Chapter 12:
Comparing Houseboats

You are probably not shopping for a houseboat, but it might have entered your mind. Plus, it's fun to think about. If you are just starting out, try a subscription to *Houseboat Magazine* by going to **www.houseboatmagazine.com** or calling 800-638-0135. Here's a quick synopsis of things you should consider.

- ☑ Recognize financing difficulties
- ☑ Discuss docking requirements
- ☑ Anticipate differing needs for bodies of water

☑ Recognize financing difficulties

First, do you have the cash to pay for one or will the seller hold the financing? It's extremely difficult to find a loan to buy a houseboat.

☑ Discuss docking requirements

Second, do you have a piece of land to which you can moor it? Houseboats accompanied by a tiny spit of land are extremely expensive. Without it, you're forced to wander, looking for places to rent (usually expensive) mooring. Along the Eastern seaboard, it's becoming increasing popular to convert public mooring to condo mooring, called dockominiums. The supply of rentable spaces is decreasing.

☑ Anticipate differing needs for bodies of water

Third, make sure the houseboat you want to buy is compatible with the body of water on which you want to place it. Some large lakes don't allow houseboats at all. Others change water levels periodically for energy generation or irrigation purposes. Your proposed mooring site could be dry land for several weeks or months. Be mindful that salt water requires different engines and systems than fresh water. Think about whether you want an engine at all—many converted barges are towed to a mooring place, where they remain.

Section III:
Construction

Chapter 13:
Selecting Land on which to Build

Many decisions that must be made when selecting land on which you plan to build your home will be the same as they would be for buying a home—what the schools are like, how far away the grocery store is, what the daily commute is going to be. When you're building, though, you have some unique concerns that must be addressed up front if you want to avoid problems later.

- ☑ Choose a location
- ☑ Consider topographic challenges
- ☑ Factor in existing vegetation
- ☑ Make sure utilities are available
- ☑ Think about the neighbors

☑ Choose a location

If you haven't already done so, read the "Location" section in Chapter 5. Add the following additional considerations to your checklists.

With subdivision lots, you need to be aware of traffic flow for vehicles involved in building new houses. Is there a separate construction entrance, or will large trucks drive past your front door at 6:00 every morning? What stage of construction are the homes next door and across the street? You could find roofers looking in your windows in the mornings and vandals turning over nearby Port-a-Potties at night.

Find out if the land is inside a city limits and if there are zoning protections. Some cities don't have zoning. Today's wooded area behind your house could be tomorrow's fertilizer plant.

What governmental authorities can assess permitting and inspection fees, and how much are they? Is there talk of an upcoming construction or sewer line moratorium, so that your land will be unbuildable for some time? How much are the environmental impact fees, if any?

In addition, think about the distance subcontractors must travel in order to perform work. Extra mileage can cause additional expenses for things like concrete and other deliveries.

For rural land, how far away is the nearest fire station, and is it volunteer or full-time? This will dramatically affect your insurance premiums.

☑ Consider topographic challenges

Topography means the contours of the land—hills and valleys—and how steep they are. A hilly site will usually be more scenic and allow you to do some interesting architectural designs. Construction will be more expensive, though, and most mail-order or standard house plans require a flat lot, unless you want to pay for modifications. Other things to consider include the following.

   ☑ How is the land situated relative to other properties?
   ☑ When it rains heavily, will all the neighbors' runoff come onto your land?
   ☑ Will the house sit on a hilltop, exposed to fierce northern winds?
   ☑ If you plan to have a lawn, will you need a lawnmower or mountain goats?

☑ Factor in existing vegetation

Another important feature when looking at vacant land is its vegetation. What sort of vegetation is present? Some parts of Houston, for example, will support tree growth. Homeowners pay extra to live in a "treed area." Maybe you'd prefer not to deal with raking leaves and picking up fallen limbs, though.

What's the quality of the vegetation already growing—does it look healthy or struggling? Ask a local nursery about the types of trees and shrubs that indicate poor soil conditions. Cedars will grow on land that would kill almost anything else. Be aware of such problems if you have grandiose landscaping plans.

Will you have to do a lot of clearing and pushing over trees in order to create a building site? Are there government or neighborhood regulations on how many trees can be cut down? As a rule of thumb, the more scenic a piece of property, the more problems it's going to cause in construction. Think about your tolerance level for problems when buying land.

☑ Make sure utilities are available

In subdivisions, find out if all utilities have been installed and if you have to pay a *tie-in* fee to connect to them. A tie-in fee is a one-time charge by the utility provider, who then rebates part of it to the developer to reimburse him or her for installing the utilities. High-speed Internet access is no longer considered a luxury—make sure your options are not limited to dial-up service or a satellite receiver. Ideally, you want fiber to the curb, or at least available DSL or cable modem service.

Raw land that is not in a subdivision might have utilities available, but that could mean spending thousands of dollars to run power or water lines to the nearest connection. Find out if you have the option of underground or above-ground power lines, and the relative cost of each. As a general rule, you'll be happier with underground service and will suffer fewer problems if you keep your lines marked. Nobody wants to accidentally cut a power line by digging in the wrong place. Determine if there's public water, and if you can secure a sewer line connection or will have to rely on a septic tank. Modern health regulations regarding septic tank engineering can add tens of thousands of dollars to your construction costs.

☑ Think about the neighbors

Most times, when you build in a subdivision, the whole community is full of newcomers. It's hard to get a sense of the neighbors except by observing their cars, bumper stickers, and the occasional children's toy. However, you can be reasonably confident that your neighbors will be homeowners with somewhat similar tastes and budgets.

Properties outside subdivisions and without zoning protections bear closer scrutiny of your surroundings. Are there feedlots or industrial operations nearby? Do the road shoulders seem to be littered with trash? Ask a surveyor if the property lines are well-settled in the area, or if the neighbors engage in constant boundary line wars. Observe how many dogs run loose, blissfully ignorant of "no trespassing" signs. Will this bother you? If you're a gardener, do you see lots of gardens nearby, indicating neighbors with common interests and welcome advice? There are a thousand and one things to look for, depending on your wants and needs. The point is to look.

Chapter 14:
Comparing Land for Construction

Ah, the excitement of building your dream home! It all starts with the land—almost anything else can be adjusted or fixed later, but you're going to be stuck with that dirt forever. Be sure to revisit Chapter 8, "Comparing Homes"—especially the sections on location and utilities. The following are some more ideas for shopping wisely.

☑ Distinguish between subdivisions and other land
☑ Find out if the current owner has a recent survey
☑ Learn about recreational and resort area restrictions
☑ Understand all about septic tanks, field lines, and perc tests
☑ Think about topographic considerations
☑ Consider unusual construction expenses

☑ Distinguish between subdivisions and other land

Lots in subdivisions are usually fairly easy to compare. Most of them already have roads and utilities in place, the land is relatively flat, and construction costs can be estimated with confidence. You'll still want to make notes about lot placement within a subdivision. Will new homes be under construction nearby, after yours is completed? This will create a noisy and dusty environment with little privacy for a while. Where is the construction entrance? Even distant home construction can cause you problems if all trucks enter the subdivision at a location near your house.

Raw land—or acreage not developed for a subdivision—introduces a lot more flexibility, independence, and anxiety over unanticipated expenses. Just be sure to make allowances for these differences when comparing the two types of properties. The ability to paint your house your school colors of blue and orange, should the mood strike you, might make raw land more attractive than a lot in a gated community. A very tight budget with no room for surprises may make subdivisions more of a focus.

☑ Find out if the current owner has a recent survey

Especially with rural lands, there's a high likelihood of confusion over the exact location of boundary lines. Large tracts of land may have been held by various family members for generations. No one ever worried about property lines, because everyone was related and on good terms. Deeds may recite "starting at the old well, go west 50 feet to a point of beginning. Thence, travel southeasterly 300 feet, more or less, to the stream bed...." None of this causes any problems until you buy your land and your lender requires a survey. Sometimes, this can result in nasty surprises for the whole area, and may dump everyone in court for decades of boundary line litigation. Take it from me—boundary line litigation *never* settles, and people will fight to the death over $1,000 worth of dirt. Rural land with a recent survey and clearly marked property corners is always more desirable than sites with indefinite boundaries.

☑ Learn about recreational and resort area restrictions

I live on a lake that provides the drinking water for my town. Because of that, any land within one mile of the lake has significant building restrictions and additional costs not imposed on other properties. There are size and type limitations for boats. Other inland waters prohibit personal watercraft, such as jet skis. In your area, nearby public lands might or might not allow snow sports, horseback riding, or many other things you thought would be permissible. As you shop, it will be important to inquire about these areas of interest.

☑ Understand all about septic tanks, field lines, and perc tests

Sewer systems are one of those things everyone takes for granted, until they're not available. If you will be a first-time resident of *exurban* (past the suburbs but before the cornfields) areas or rural land, make sure you compare the existence and quality of septic tanks, field lines, and perc tests. According to the American Ground Water Trust, approximately 28% of American homes have septic tanks. That means it's very likely you will look at a home with such a system.

Septic tanks hold household waste water. Heavy solids sink to the bottom of the tank, while lighter materials form a scummy crust that is digested by microorganisms. Liquids pass out of the tank into underground tubing with tiny holes, called *field lines*. The tank has to be pumped every few years in order to remove accumulated solids from the bottom. The *field lines* allow slow and steady drainage of water and partially digested liquids into an area called the *drainfield*. Discharge seeps through a gravel bed and soil saturated with more microbes, providing the final cleansing. The ability of the soil to percolate, or allow easy transmission of water through the layers, is critical to the proper functioning of a septic system. The test for this is called a *perc* (pronounced "perk") test.

Knowing all of that, this is what you need to compare. First, is the property connected to a public sewer or can you tie in at a nearby location? What does it cost to tie in to the sewer system? This can be extremely expensive. If there is no public sewer, is there a septic tank in place? How old is it and when was the last time it was pumped out? How many problems has the owner had with the septic tank? Does it include a grinder pump to grind up solids and then pump them to another holding tank? If there's a grinder pump, is it a dual pump that switches over if one pump goes out, giving you time to obtain repairs? Otherwise, when the grinder pump fails, all the water has to stop running or your tank will flood. Where are the field lines? If there are trees or large shrubs growing there, your field lines will be clogged with roots and the whole system will eventually fail, backing sewage up into the home. Find out if local health regulations changed, so you'll be required to install a new system even if the old one is working well. Finally, you sometimes encounter a health department septic tank moratorium—no new permits will be issued for an indefinite period of time. If that happens, you won't be able to build and your land will be practically worthless to you.

Be sure to ask about recent perc tests and make notes about the results. Even if the prior owner has had a trouble-free septic system for years, you should never buy such land without a new perc test. Smart, motivated owners will have one on hand for your inspection. Less sophisticated sellers might not think to provide this, so you should include it as a contract contingency.

This might seem like a lot of space devoted to septic tanks, but it's pretty important. If you can't flush the toilet, just about every other wonderful thing about your home will seem pale and worthless.

☑ Think about topographic considerations

Topography refers to the contours of land. Flat land with a known subsurface of clay is the easiest to build on. Hilltops usually have the best views, but you generally have to blast through rock in order to create flat surfaces. In addition, the home is subject to frigid northern winds, blasting heat from the summer sun, and treacherous driveway conditions during rain, snow, or icy conditions. Wooded glades in the hollows between two hills will be cool in the summer, picturesque year-round, but subject to damage from falling trees. Cold air will settle there in the winter, trapped even on warm, sunny days. Make notes about these things, think about how they will impact you, and choose accordingly.

☑ Consider unusual construction expenses

Some properties are better suited for construction than others. The more difficult ones will take longer and be far more expensive than you ever thought. Topography enters into this, because irregularly shaped land has to be flattened or the house plan has to be adapted to the land contours. If your site is hilly, you may need to hire a pumper truck for concrete work, or pay hourly workers to cart concrete up or down a hill.

If your property is located some distance from the major construction suppliers, delivery expenses will be higher. Due to security and weather problems, construction materials are not delivered to a job site all at once. They arrive almost daily, in small batches. You may have delivery surcharges each time, or you may simply pay a higher unit cost for materials and increased hourly rate for labor. In addition, many subcontractors pay their hourly workers for commuting time one-way. Every hour your three-person plumbing crew spends on the road is three man-hours you pay for, but obtain no work.

Rapidly growing communities, or even ones that want to avoid rapid growth, impose large impact fees for new construction. This is to compensate the community for increased fire and police protection, possible school expenses, or other services necessary when there is residential growth. Environmentally sensitive locations may require environmental impact reports before a building permit will be issued.

Utilities are always important. How far is the nearest power and public water, and how much will it cost to run service out to your home site? If there are many trees, will you want to choose underground power, which is still more expensive? Will the trees interfere with satellite, television, or Internet services that require a clear southern exposure? Do you think you'll need a backup generator? Comparing all of these factors may make some properties more desirable than others, and some apparently wonderful sites will become totally unrealistic.

If in doubt about other unusual construction expenses, check with any local planning and zoning or inspections departments. They can usually provide you with good background information or refer you to other experts.

Chapter 15:
Working with a Contractor or Construction Company

Building your own home can be a wonderful and rewarding experience, or it can drive you into bankruptcy and prescription medications. You tilt the scales in your favor by being prepared and avoiding the most common pitfalls.

- ☑ Choose the right level of construction supervision
- ☑ Select three construction professionals to interview
- ☑ Do a background check
- ☑ Understand your lender's construction policies
- ☑ Manage the planning meeting
- ☑ Prepare a construction budget
- ☑ Understand change orders—a trap for the unwary
- ☑ Sign a contract
- ☑ Inspect what you expect

☑ Choose the right level of construction supervision

When working with a contractor or construction company, you have many choices regarding levels of supervision. Unfortunately, many people don't realize this until it's too late. They sign a contract that gives them less protection, less control, or more responsibility than they thought. Don't make the same mistake.

The most common relationship is with a developer who builds a subdivision of roughly similar homes. The developer offers firm prices, fairly predictable completion dates, and closing when the home is completed. The developer controls everything and supervises all subcontractors. You will not be allowed to recommend your brother-in-law for the plumbing work, and you may be barred from the construction site if you become a pest. You will be given a budget for certain items you may customize—paint and wallpaper, carpeting, plumbing, and lighting fixtures. The developer will tell you that if you save money in one area, such as more economical carpeting, you can usually spend it on something else, such as nicer plumbing fixtures. In the real world, this rarely happens. The budget usually contemplates the cheapest possible materials and labor.

Other contractors will build a home to a certain stage and then turn it over to you for completion. Usually, this involves *getting the house in the black*, meaning all the framing is done and the roof covered with roofing felt, which is typically black. You will then be responsible for hiring, supervising, and paying plumbers, electricians, roofers, and others. Be sure you have a firm understanding of construction work before embarking on such a relationship, because there could be many surprises to your budget. You also want to obtain an itemized list of the work to be completed by the contractor, and a good faith estimate of the scope and cost of items that will be your responsibility.

Custom homes can be built on a fixed-cost basis, or a cost-plus-profit basis. A *general contractor* will be responsible for obtaining the best prices and supervising all subcontractors to make sure they perform their work properly. At the other extreme is a *construction manager*, who will schedule work crews in the right order, but is not legally responsible for securing the best bids or supervising the work. Beware of such a relationship—it may seem like the construction manager is in control, but he or she has very few legal responsibilities if something goes wrong.

☑ Select three construction professionals to interview

Ask for builder recommendations from your lender or mortgage broker, the supervisor of the local construction inspections office, and two or three large subcontractors, such as HVAC, plumbing, or electrical. Be sure to mention the price range of the home you want to build. All the listed people will be knowledgeable enough to recommend a few choices. In addition, ask all your normal sources from whom you obtain recommendations. You'll probably start to see several names popping up on everyone's lists. Those are the ones you want to interview.

You may have to make several phone calls before you find builders willing to take new work. Experienced construction professionals are too smart to take on more work than they can properly manage. Once you have three choices, set up interview meetings and ask questions about the following areas.

- ☑ Experience with homes similar to yours—not in general
- ☑ References of completed and under-construction homes, as well as a bank reference and some supplier references for creditworthiness
- ☑ Name of insurance agent for liability and workers' compensation

☑ Types of crews on payroll and equipment on hand
☑ Ability to prepare construction cost estimates
☑ Method of compensation, exactly, with examples
☑ Internal expenses that will be charged to you
☑ Frequency of payment for self and subcontractors
☑ Ability to accept your job and complete on time and in budget
☑ Reason you should chose this person rather than another contractor

Insider trick: Contractors

You stand the highest likelihood of having construction problems if you have a contractor with money problems. Asking about supplier and bank references will help flush this out, but you also have to check those references. In addition, a contractor who can't give you an insurance agent's name is operating on the fringes and should not be hired. Virtually every contractor has at least a few employees—such as an office assistant, clean-up crew, perhaps some carpentry crews—who will require workers' compensation insurance. At the very least, the contractor should have liability insurance, or you shouldn't hire him or her!

☑ Do a background check

After choosing the right kind of relationship and selecting a contractor, check him or her out. Ask for the names of other houses or subdivisions he or she has completed over the course of the past five years. Visit the older ones first. Meet some of the homeowners and talk to them. Most problems associated with shoddy construction techniques start showing up within two to five years.

Go to your local courthouse and ask for assistance in finding any liens or lawsuits against your contractor. Visit the construction inspections department of your city or town to find out if the contractor failed any inspections recently. See if there are any complaints filed with the Better Business Bureau.

If you've already selected a construction lender, chat with the loan officer about his or her knowledge of the contractor. The loan officer will be diplomatic but truthful—a problem contractor is going to make problems for the loan officer, too.

☑ Understand your lender's construction policies

You should have a lender in mind before you begin interviewing contractors. The loan officer will be invaluable in providing insight and advice in the selection process. In addition, the lender's requirements and fee schedules may not be compatible with some builders. For example, a contractor might require you to make payments whenever a bill is presented by the various suppliers and subcontractors. This could be dozens of checks a month. However, your lender may charge a fee for every one of these *draw requests*, so you would be better off writing checks only once a month. Some lenders will provide funds only after the loan officer performs an inspection, for which there might be a fee or even significant delays.

Most homeowners will obtain a loan package called a *construction-to-permanent loan*. It's actually two loans—a construction loan (with special terms, a short maturity date, and higher interest rate) and conversion-to-permanent financing just like any other new home mortgage. You could lose your automatic conversion if the house is not completed on time or if it goes over budget without lender approvals for the change orders. If you lose your conversion, you will have to shop for permanent financing, interest rates may be higher, and you will certainly have to pay loan closing expenses for a second time. There are many loan-related variables when building a home. Make sure you have a clear understanding of all requirements, so you can discuss them with the builder.

☑ Manage the planning meeting

Meet with your builder to go over all details of construction, timing, payment, and responsibilities. Bring a tape recorder with you. The tiniest detail—the one you forget to make a note about—will usually be the one to cause problems in the future. Discuss any requirements your lender has, and make sure the builder is agreeable to working with them.

If available at the time of the first meeting, have your wish list of carpet, wallpaper, plumbing, lighting fixtures, and appliances, together with their prices. Ask if those items can be included within the agreed price or will cost extra. Obtain an agreement that you will be supplied with a construction timetable, a schedule of inspections and payments, and a line-item budget (or *takeoff*) for the various aspects of construction. Pointedly ask these questions: "Exactly what are my responsibilities?" and "Is everything else your responsibility?" If the builder won't answer, but wants you to simply refer to the contract, run like crazy and thank your lucky stars you avoided a bad mistake.

Make sure you can come on the construction site as often as you want, as long as you're not in the way, in order to inspect progress. Many construction mistakes are covered up by drywall, carpet, or trim work before anyone can learn about them.

Afterwards, make a copy of the tape recording. You want to attach it to the construction contract. In addition, listen to the recording later and make detailed notes. Refer back to them often to make sure things are going as originally discussed.

☑ Prepare a construction budget

You can do your own construction estimating with easily available software. A good source is **www.craftsman-books.com**, where you can download a thirty-day free trial of their software. The full version, with a book, is less than $60. Your local bookstore or online bookseller will have a wide variety of books and software. Find one that feels comfortable to you.

If you are entering a cost-plus contract rather than a firm-price contract, it is essential that you have a good idea regarding the cost of your home before you ask the builder for his or her construction budget. That way, you'll have an early warning if the contractor's budget is way off base.

Next, obtain the contractor's takeoffs, if possible. Many custom home builders will not prepare the detailed budget until you've signed a contract. There's a lot of work involved if done properly. It's easier with a semi-custom home. If the builder has given you an estimate of construction costs, but won't prepare a budget before you have a contract, ask to see a home that cost a similar amount, per square foot, to build. Notice the quality of the following items.

☑ Flooring—carpet (weight less than thirty-five ounces will not hold up well), wood, tile, vinyl

☑ Light fixtures

☑ Plumbing fixtures

☑ Wall finishes—all paint or some wallpaper

☑ Cabinetry—wood, vinyl laminate, full extension drawers, lauan (cheap) drawer bottoms

☑ Countertops—tile, granite, synthetic stone, laminate

☑ Shelving—wood or coated wire

☑ Windows—energy efficient, easy clean, fixed or open, number

☑ Garage doors—metal or wood, number, openers, windows
in doors

☑ Landscaping—minimal, none, adequate, irrigation system

Is the quality of these items similar to what you were expecting in your home? If not, go back to the drawing board to make a budget, check out some other builders, or adjust your expectations regarding the home you will be able to afford.

☑ Understand change orders— a trap for the unwary

If you are given a budget or a firm price for a home, it will be based on a specific set of plans, finishes, and a schedule. Any variances will cost significantly more money. It is common for homeowners to request a large number of very minor changes without being aware of the expense involved. Although it might cost $2,000 to wire an entire house, it might cost a per-item *flat rate* of $65 each—$650—to add only ten extra outlets. If added to the original plans before the electrician bid the job, those additional outlets might have added only $100 to the cost. That's because change orders are viewed as easy additional income. Many subcontractors bid jobs at break-even or a small loss, so they can beat out the other bidders and get the job. They rely on change orders to supply the profit. To be fair, changes do break up the flow of things, so construction does not go as smoothly and effortlessly as planned. That has an impact on the price structure.

Be sure that you and your builder have a firm policy that no changes will be allowed unless requested by you in writing, with a firm price for the change order included in that document. Most reputable builders have preprinted forms for this. Your policy should be—if it is not signed and in writing, then there will be no payment, no argument. Do not depart from this policy under any circumstances! Otherwise, you will be stunned to discover things claimed as change orders that you never authorized, didn't realize would cost more money, or were not changes at all but requests for a subcontractor to correct his or her own mistakes.

☑ Sign a contract

Don't enter into any relationship to build a house unless you have a written contract with details about responsibilities, payment, scheduling, change orders, and what happens if there's a dispute. Don't sign until you can read the contract thoroughly and obtain advice from someone else.

Most builders' contracts require arbitration to resolve conflicts. Although this is enticing because of the simplified process and speedy schedules, it rarely works out to the consumer's advantage. The arbitrator can't be overruled on appeal, even if he or she makes obvious mistakes in the law. As an alternative, suggest your willingness to have a nonjury trial, thereby allaying builder concerns about runaway juries awarding millions for minor acts of negligence.

Read the contract thoroughly and ask questions about anything that doesn't make sense to you. It's a good idea to tape-record that meeting, also. Ask for a provision giving you the right to inspect the builder's books and make sure all subcontractors and suppliers are being paid on a timely basis. Although you might pay all draw requests promptly, a builder in trouble might use that money for other things, instead of paying your plumber, electrician, concrete company, etc. Those unpaid people will file liens against the property. You will have to pay off the liens, and then chase the contractor for reimbursement. Usually, these situations don't have a happy ending.

How it works in the real world: Lender Construction Rules

Your lender will probably require the builder to supply lien releases before construction draws will be paid. The loan documents may also prohibit payments unless the project passes certain inspections confirming the progress of construction. These things are meant to protect the lender, not you. If the loan officer gets sloppy and doesn't obtain lien releases or doesn't perform inspections, you might use up all your construction money and then discover a sloppy or dishonest builder didn't use your money on your home. The house could be only half-finished, with dozens of liens filed against it by subcontractors. You won't be able to sue the lender for poor oversight, because the lender did not owe you any oversight responsibilities. You will have to monitor the draw request process yourself.

Make sure the contract spells out the builder's warranties and how long they will last. One year is typical. In addition, you should have a certain period of time after completion to identify *punch list* items—minor repairs or completions—that will be performed at no charge. A squeaky floor may be covered by the warranty, but the accidental omission of switch plates is just too bad, unless you have a punch list clause. Usually, you will be given an appointment for a walk-through, during which you must identify all punch list items. Insist on a period of at least two weeks after you begin occupancy, not just one trip. A lot can be overlooked in that one appointment.

Before signing, ask someone you trust to review the contract for comments and suggestions. It's preferable that the person be someone who's built a house in the past. In addition, ask your lender or mortgage broker for advice, and assurance that the contract will not conflict with any of your loan provisions or cost you additional fees.

☑ Inspect what you expect

Don't make a pest of yourself, but the squeaky wheel does get the grease, after all. Visit the job site as often as you can in order to review the progress and quality of the work. Even if you know nothing about construction techniques, you can tell some things. Are materials left out in the open, subject to weather damage or theft? You might think you don't care, because you have a fixed-price contract. On the other hand, a builder who suffers the loss of several thousand dollars in lumber will not absorb it. Instead, he or she will cut corners somewhere on your house in order to make it up. Find out when inspections are scheduled and then be present, or ask for proof the inspection was passed. Failed inspections cause delays, and delays cost money. If possible, ensure that suppliers and sub-contractors are being paid on a timely basis. Listen to the workers talking. There's usually a good bit of animosity among plumbers, electricians, carpenters, etc., because each feels the other is in the way. They'll complain about each other a lot. Pay attention—you might learn about some problems and be able to have them repaired.

Chapter 16:

Specifying Finishes and Fixtures in a New Home

Many subdivision homes are built as *spec homes*. The builder hopes to have a buyer shortly before completion of construction. The buyer is then able to choose his or her own paint, wallpaper, plumbing, lighting fixtures, and sometimes flooring and cabinetry. Typically, the builder will give you a budget for each area. Savings on some items can be spent on other things, as long as you stay within the total budget or are willing to pay extra. The choices generally come at the end of construction, when you're tired and anxious for completion. Failure to be careful can blow your whole budget.

The list of your preferences is called the *finish schedule*. Your written finish schedule is vitally important to clear communication, having the house you want, and no surprises in the area of money.

- ☑ Determine if you can specify finishes and fixtures
- ☑ Obtain a budget and schedule from the builder
- ☑ Make wise choices
- ☑ Put your finish schedule in writing

☑ Determine if you can specify finishes and fixtures

A few builders won't let you make any changes—not even in a paint color. They buy Adobe White paint in fifty-five-gallon drums, work on tight schedules, and can't afford the time to obtain paint and supplies necessary to make your home all the colors of the rainbow. Find out early if this is the case.

☑ Obtain a budget and schedule from the builder

Fortunately, most contractors will allow you to specify some details. Be sure to obtain a written list of the items you can select, and the allowance you have to work with. If this is provided to you verbally, write everything down and ask the builder to sign it. A little extra work on the front end can save many misunderstandings and a possible lawsuit on the back end.

Ask for some examples of the kinds of things that can be purchased within the budget. Most consumers lack an understanding of construction expenses. What seems like a generous budget for cabinets might buy only chipboard pre-fab units with fake wood surfaces and the cheapest possible pulls and handles. Ask hardware suppliers about extras. Tub drains, sink strainers, door hinges, and cabinet pulls are usually overlooked but add expenses. If you are buying a home in an upscale community, and the countertop budget will permit only Formica rather than tile or granite, that may not be acceptable to you. It's good to get an early warning that the home of your dreams will have compromises, or will cost additional money.

You also need to know a schedule of deadlines for making decisions. Some must be made earlier than others because everything has to be timed exactly right during the last few weeks of construction. Changing countertops from Formica® to granite might mean the cabinets or floor must be reinforced because of the additional weight. Missing a deadline for specifying a finish could mean you'll have to execute a change order—and pay extra—for your choice, even if nothing has to be ripped out or redone.

☑ Make wise choices

Sometimes we have to make sacrifices to save money. Think about the strategically best places to cut corners—where it won't show and won't compromise overall quality. Think about things that will be cheap or easy to replace later, or can be omitted entirely for awhile.

If you need to compromise on quality somewhere, go with the inexpensive lights. Cap the wiring for the ceiling fans and buy them later. Do buy the wallpaper you want for the bathrooms and kitchens, with all their intricate cuts that make it hard for do-it-yourselfers. Just paint the large rectangular walls that will be easy to paper later. By the way—make absolutely certain the drywall has an initial coat of primer paint before hanging wallpaper, especially if you plan to replace it later. Many paperhangers omit this step. As a result, when you attempt to remove the old paper, big chunks of drywall come off at the same time.

Sometimes you might want to omit some things entirely rather than complete them inexpensively and then tear out and redo later. If you can't afford hardwood floors right now, maybe you can leave them in cement or lauan subfloor and just put down an oriental rug to hide the "ugly." Think about a kitchen with painted flea-market china cabinets and open shelving until you're ready for custom cabinets. It's considered quite fashionable, and saves all that wasted money on stock cabinets that will end up at the town dump when you remodel.

☑ Put your finish schedule in writing

This is one of those areas that is prone to miscommunication. List each room separately and identify it by location within the home. "Laura's bedroom" means nothing to a painter, but "SE bedroom on ground floor, next to the stairs" communicates a thought he or she can work with. Detail every choice within each room. Don't rely on a master instruction such as "all walls will be Sherwin Williams #1234—Chili Pepper Red—unless otherwise specified." Be precise about model numbers, manufacturers, prices, color numbers, and add-on features. Remember that cabinets and drawers don't come with pulls, handles, or hinges, so you'll have to choose those, also. Sinks and faucets don't arrive with drains, and toilet seats have to be purchased separately from toilets. Something as simple as lightbulbs can add hundreds of dollars to a home if you select fixtures that require specialty bulbs. If in doubt about necessary add-ons, ask a supplier for advice.

Once you have your written finish schedule and an agreement regarding pricing, make two copies. Have your contractor sign the original and give it back to you, and keep it in a safe place. Give one copy to the contractor so he or she can take care of completion. Keep the other copy in your car for ready reference as you visit the site or shop for accessories.

Section IV:
Contracts

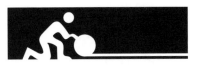

Chapter 17:
Preparing an Offer

Making an offer on a home involves more than just specifying a dollar amount you are willing to pay. If you take the time to think about some of the other details, you can save yourself a lot of grief and possible expense down the road. Your offer should address each of the points discussed in this chapter.

- ☑ Find out if there is a widely used form contract in the community
- ☑ Remember—everything is negotiable
- ☑ Pay attention to seemingly unimportant details
- ☑ Spell out important monetary terms
- ☑ Specify exactly what you're buying and when
- ☑ Require the seller to provide you with certain documents before closing
- ☑ List circumstances that will allow you to cancel the contract without penalty
- ☑ Be specific about allocating closing expenses and prorates
- ☑ Prepare for the worst—what happens if someone defaults

It must be in writing because it cuts down on confusion regarding what you meant to offer; real estate agents in most states must immediately relay written offers to their clients, but verbal offers have more latitude; if the seller wants to accept your offer, her or she simply has to sign; and, most contracts related to real estate must be in writing to be enforceable. If you only have conversations, then someone must take more time and draft an actual contract.

☑ Find out if there is a widely used form contract in the community

If you are working with a real estate agent, that agent will have a *form* real estate contract that he or she would like you to use in preparation of an offer. Buyers without the assistance of an agent will usually encounter a selling agent who wants you to use his or her form contract. Almost all real estate forms in a community are virtually identical. Everyone is familiar and comfortable with them. Attempting to use a do-it-yourself contract adds an element of uncertainty and mild distrust. On the other hand, you can modify the form contract as much as you want. It does not make sense, but you can mark up a five-page form as much as you want and it will be more palatable than a one-page, plain-English contract that you write from scratch. For those of you working with FSBO sellers, you'll need to obtain a form contract. State laws vary widely, so it's difficult to put a model contract in this book. Visit **www.uslegalforms.com** or call them at 877-389-0141 to obtain something tailored for your state. Make sure you ask a local attorney for advice to make sure the contract complies with all state laws.

☑ Remember—everything is negotiable

There are only a few requirements for a legally binding real estate contract. You must name the seller, name the buyer, supply the legal description of the property, name a price, and include some language saying, in effect, "seller agrees to sell and buyer agrees to buy." It must be in writing and signed by all parties. Some states require certain disclosures, while others give cancellation rights to buyers or sellers. Omitting these items doesn't make the contract unenforceable, it just modifies the parties' understanding of when they can back out of the deal.

Everything else is negotiable. If you want the seller to pay all the closing costs, put that in your offer. Would you like to move into the house three weeks before closing? Throw it out there in the offer. Whatever you might have heard about how things are usually done is just that—how things are *usually* done.

☑ Pay attention to seemingly unimportant details

If you have a form to use, read every word and ask questions about what the clauses mean. Some things that are common overlooked, but can have important consequences, include the following.

- Full names and marital status for seller and buyer. Don't use nicknames. Include "Jr." and other such modifiers, even if rarely used in your signature. Because of homestead or community property rights, some states require disclosure of marital status on all deeds. Women who have been married less than ten years should include their maiden names and married name, if different, to make title checks easier. All of this information is important to the title insurance company for a timely completion of their work.

- Legal description and street address of the property, and approximate size of land. Many times, a contract is not enforceable if it contains only a street address. Obtain the legal description from the seller's deed, or from the tax assessor's office. Include the street address in case there is a mistake in the legal description—the street address can help clarify what the parties intended. The approximate size of the parcel will prevent mistakes about what's being sold. If the seller has a double lot, are you buying both lots or just the one with the house sitting on it? If buying acreage, do you want the thirty-nine acres that forms the majority of the place, or the thirty-nine acres plus the one acre on which the house sits? In the real world, such mistakes happen often and people are left with less than they intended to purchase.

☑ Spell out important monetary terms

Be as precise as possible about these details. They are the most frequent cause of misperceptions and contract disputes.

The price is what everyone thinks about first. There's rarely any confusion, but do spell out the amount in addition to writing the numerals. Someone might mistake $125,000 for $175,000 under some circumstances, but there's no mistake about the additional language, "one hundred twenty-five thousand dollars and no cents."

There's an additional problem most people will never encounter, but it's sometimes interesting to talk about with friends, so you sound knowledgeable. What happens if the purchase price is expressed in Canadian dollars, and the exchange rate changes between contract signing and closing? Which date's exchange rate do you use? The contract has to specify, or there will be a mess.

You should also spell out the terms—including if it's all-cash or seller financing. It's not enough to propose an offer with seller financing. You have to spell out the details of the financing. Otherwise, that portion of the contract could be unenforceable because it lacks specificity in the eyes of the law. Include the interest rate, amount financed, length of the loan—such as twenty years, thirty years, balloon after five years—and frequency of payments (monthly, for example). (Read Chapter 20 for more information on seller financing.)

Contracts require something called *consideration*. This usually means a promise exchanged for a promise. The seller promised to sell and you promised to buy. However, most sellers want you to put down some earnest money, even though it is not required for a legally binding contract. It shows you have the probable ability to secure the financing to close. It also provides *hostage value* in case you decide to breach the contract. You should spell out the amount of earnest money, as well as who will hold it. Usually this is an escrow company or sometimes the seller's real estate agent. The seller should never be allowed to keep the earnest money in his or her own account.

☑ Specify exactly what you're buying and when

Decide what things will be included in the sale besides the real estate, and how much time you will have to complete all your pre-closing inspections and other tasks. Take the following things into consideration.

☑ *Personal property included in sale.* What items of personal property will remain behind? Most common items are swing sets, window coverings, appliances, and garage door openers. Don't forget about decorative flowerbed edging, the mailbox, and the lightbulbs. Sometimes buyers include in an offer that the sellers leave behind something unique, such as antique furniture or decorations, and the seller agrees. If there's something that's important, like a crystal chandelier or custom front door, include it in the contract. Such things might *technically* be part of the real estate in your state and automatically included. However, do you really want to hire a lawyer and fight about it afterwards? Put it in black and white in the offer.

☑ *Time and date of closing.* When does closing have to take place? Include wording such as "on or before thirty days from full execution of a sale contract." Make sure you can finalize all arrangements, including your loan, in that time period. If you don't close, you'll be in default and could forfeit your earnest money *and* be liable for additional damages. Inclusion of the words "time is of the essence" in a contract usually means you will not be given any leeway about missed deadlines. If those magic words are missing, a court might say you were not in default if you were late. However, you don't really want a court making those decisions. Give yourself enough time to do everything. It doesn't have to be thirty days—it can be any time period the parties agree to.

☑ *Risk of loss.* Who has the *risk of loss*? This is always specified as the seller, but you have to say so. Otherwise, if the house burns to the ground and there's no insurance, you may still have to buy the property. If there is an insurable loss right before closing, can you elect to take the insurance proceeds, go through with closing, and then rebuild the way you want to? If you want to do this, say so in the offer.

☑ *Seller move-out.* When will the seller move out? Ideally this would be on the day before closing, so you can do your final walk-through (see page 205) before closing. Some sellers want to negotiate for a later move-out date. If you are agreeable, require a written lease, a security deposit, and some amount of rent, just in case you have to evict them.

☑ Require the seller to provide you with certain documents before closing

You will want to review some documents before making a final decision to go forward with closing. Be sure to list things you want the seller to provide, and give yourself a specific time period to cancel the contract without penalty if you find something objectionable. If available, describe the following things in your offer:

- ☑ survey—a survey may show boundaries in a different place than the parties thought, and it may show a boundary line in a different place than where a fence or hedge line currently sits, indicating potential problems;
- ☑ recent appraisal—the seller may have obtained an appraisal for insurance purposes or in preparation to sell the property;
- ☑ recent wood infestation and moisture report;
- ☑ condo association minutes and budgets—you want to discover any surprises that will make ownership more difficult or expensive than you originally thought;
- ☑ homeowners association restrictions and budget; and,
- ☑ warranties covering any major household systems.

☑ List circumstances that will allow you to cancel the contract without penalty

If you can cancel a contract if certain described things either do or do not happen, those are called *contingencies*. Examples would include cancellation if a home inspector says the house will need over $1,000 in repairs or if you find anything in the documents discussed in the previous section that disturbs you. An example of a cancellation if something *does not* happen is a contingency for acceptable financing—if you cannot obtain financing on acceptable terms, you can cancel the contract. None of these things happen automatically. You only have the contingencies the parties agree to, and no others—with one exception. Some states have seller disclosure laws that allow a buyer to cancel a contract if the legally required disclosures reveal unacceptable defects. Possible contingencies include:

- ☑ a failed home inspection;
- ☑ a home inspection recommending more than a certain dollar amount in repairs;
- ☑ a failed termite inspection;
- ☑ dissatisfaction with matters revealed by documents produced by seller;
- ☑ failure of seller to produce documents previously agreed upon;
- ☑ your inability to obtain acceptable financing (although prudent sellers will not leave this so open-ended as to allow you to decide what's acceptable or not. They might limit such a contingency to certain interest rates, or they might give you a very short period of time to obtain a loan commitment or THEY can cancel the contract);
- ☑ the lender's appraisal being less than the purchase price;
- ☑ your inability to get out of a lease;
- ☑ your inability to sell another home (you might have inherited a home and this truly is the first time you are buying one);
- ☑ if you or your spouse are active or inactive military and called up for service elsewhere;
- ☑ the seller's inability to deliver clean title with no liens; and
- ☑ anything else acceptable to both parties.

☑ Be specific about allocating closing expenses and prorates

Closing expenses are things like the title insurance fee, attorney's fee, document preparation, and recording fees. Prorates cover expenses that have been paid in advance by the seller but provide benefits extending into your time of ownership, or expenses that you will pay in the future but will cover time periods during which the seller owned the property.

Homeowner's association or condo fees are generally paid in advance, so you might be expected to reimburse the seller for some portion of that expense. Property taxes are usually paid at the end of the fiscal year, so you might expect the seller to reimburse you for that bill. There are no hard and fast rules about how to divide these things—you should spell them out in your offer. In the list below a statement about what is customary in most markets is included.

☑ Owner's title insurance is handled many ways. Sometimes the seller pays it, sometimes the buyer, sometimes they each pay half.

☑ Lender's title insurance is usually paid by the buyer, because he or she is the borrower and the one who caused that particular expense.

☑ Closing fees charged by the closing company are usually paid half each, including any overnight delivery charges and wire transfer fees.

☑ Attorney's fees may be separate from the closing fees. Each party usually pays half.

☑ Document preparation for everything associated with the deed is usually paid half by each. Document preparation for loan documents is usually paid by the buyer, but sometimes the parties agree to pay half each. This is usually a relatively small number.

☑ Transfer taxes may be paid by seller or buyer, depending on the community and the laws regarding those taxes. This can be a large sum of money.

☑ Recordation fees are usually paid by the buyer. This can be very large.

☑ There might be condo association assessments for long overdue repairs or government assessments for road or utility work to be performed in the future. Most form contracts says the seller pays for any assessments imposed before closing and the buyer pays for anything imposed after closing. The better practice would be to do some research regarding who really received the benefit of the work represented by the assessment, and have that person pay the bill. As a practical matter, there's usually no way to figure this out before making an offer, so people just use the form language.

☑ Prepare for the worst—what happens if someone defaults

Sometimes people find themselves unable or unwilling to honor their contractual commitments. You might discover a house defect previously unanticipated, but that causes you to change your mind about buying. Perhaps it's haunted, or the neighbors are drug dealers, or most of the front yard will be taken by the state for road expansion. Likewise, the seller might change his or her mind and decide not to sell to anyone at all. You'll need to include a clause to spell out the actions if this happens in your offer. The following are some possibilities.

> ☑ If the buyer defaults, he or she can forfeit the earnest money but have no other liability. Legally, you could be liable for a lot more money unless you specify just the earnest money.

> ☑ If the buyer defaults, he or she will forfeit the earnest money and be liable for damages. Sellers want such a clause, but you should object to this. In some states, a defaulting party who loses a lawsuit is also responsible for the other person's legal fees. In other states, you have to spell this out in the contract.

> ☑ If the seller defaults, you should provide for the ability to obtain *specific performance* by obtaining a court order requiring the sale to go forward. Be sure to include something making the seller responsible for your legal fees.

☑ Sellers usually want a clause saying they have to pay a small penalty, called *liquidated damages*, in case they default, but nothing additional. Object to such a clause. If you are not successful, make the liquidated damages as least as large as your earnest money.

If anything else is important to you about the property or the deal, be sure to mention it in your offer and obtain clear agreement on those terms. Even if the seller is a relative or a good friend, treat the transaction exactly as you would if dealing with a stranger. Many long-standing friendships have been destroyed over misremembered or misunderstood verbal contracts. Too many families have been separated into bitter factions because of a house sale that resulted in unexpected problems. When dealing with friends and family, explain that it's not a matter of trust when it comes to contracts. It's an issue of clear communications. Remember that fact when it comes to all contracts, and you'll be fine.

Chapter 18:

Hiring a Home Inspector

Even with new construction, it is extremely important that you have a home inspection done. A good home inspection can save you hundreds or even thousands of dollars. It can prevent a financially fatal buying mistake.

With a new home, there's no one to share their experiences with you about any problems. Everything is unknown, and problems might not become visible until after expiration of the new home warranty. Even with a report of "All fine—no defects at all," you can still use the opportunity to ask advice about preventing future problems. When hiring a home inspector, do the following.

- ☑ Order property reports to assist your inspector
- ☑ Obtain the names of three inspectors to interview
- ☑ Do a phone interview and ask for sample reports
- ☑ Check scheduling, turnaround time, and fees
- ☑ Make your choice and be present during the inspection

☑ Order property reports to assist your inspector

Everyone makes mistakes. Any information you can give a home inspector to provide an advance notice of potential problems will benefit you. To that end, call the local building inspections department and ask about any building or repair permits on the property over the course of the last five years. These may lead to other questions, such as "Why did you need to rebuild the garage last year—was there a fire?" Contact the health department about septic tank or sewer line inspections, and the gas company about gas line leak inspections. Request copies of the water bills for the last year. Unusually high bills may indicate broken or leaking water lines. Go to the courthouse and check the public records to see if the homeowner sued anyone for improper home repairs, or if someone sued the homeowner for unpaid repair bills.

You can order insurance claim reports from a company called ChoicePoint. Go online to **www.choicetrust.com**, then click on "C.L.U.E. reports." You can also call 866-312-8076 and speak with a representative. If there have been any insured losses for the property within the last five years, they will appear on the report. It might make a difference to your buying decision or the type of home inspector you hire if you knew the house had a catastrophic fire loss nine months earlier.

☑ Obtain the names of three inspectors to interview

Ask the real estate agent or mortgage broker for the names of three inspectors to interview, but take their recommendations with a grain of salt. Remember, if you don't buy the home, they don't get paid. It's not in their best interest to recommend a tough inspector to you.

The most common areas requiring repairs before closing are plumbing, HVAC (heating, ventilation, and air conditioning), and electrical. Those contractors love tough inspectors. Call a few plumbers and ask them to recommend a really thorough inspector.

Finally, check local directories for inspectors with informative ads. Find someone with licensing credentials, several years of experience, and a willingness to provide the names of buyers as references.

☑ Do a phone interview and ask for sample reports

Aside from licensing and experience, you also want to get a sense of how tough the inspector will be. You'll ask, "Tell me about a sale that fell apart because of your findings." Beware of anyone who's never had a sale fall through because of a failed inspection. Then ask, "What are the most common problems and how expensive are they to fix, generally?" and "What other inspections do you recommend I obtain?" Be suspicious of an inspector who says he or she can do everything. Sometimes cracks in the brick might be noticed by the general inspector, but require checking out by a structural engineer, who will charge an additional fee. There may be other examples. Find out your inspector's philosophy about being able to handle all your inspections, and then evaluate whether you trust him or her or not.

Ask each candidate for a sample report for an inspection with severe problems, and a sample for a relatively clean inspection. Read them to see what clues they give you about the inspector, the process, or things you should be wary about when shopping.

☑ Check scheduling, turnaround time, and fees

It won't matter that you've found the perfect inspector if he or she can't help you until next summer and the report will take six weeks to generate. Ask if the inspector is taking new work, how much notice he or she needs to fit you into his or her schedule, and how long after inspection you can expect the report. Inquire about pricing, things that might cause the price to increase, and additional charges for putting a rush on an inspection. A company with a *rush surcharge* policy is prepared to take last-minute orders. That's good to know, in case you need to move quickly for some reason. Other inspectors might simply tell you they can't help you if you give them insufficient notice. Finally, ask if the inspector must be paid in advance, when the report is delivered, or at closing. An inspector who's paid at closing has a vested interest in closing taking place—just like a real estate agent. It might tip the scales towards selecting someone else.

☑ Make your choice and be present during the inspection

Once you choose an inspector, make sure you have some sort of writing that spells out your agreement. It might be a form contract provided by the inspector, an *order for services*, or even just a letter you write up. The most critical terms are timing, cost, and scope of inspection—what is included and what is excluded. If not already present on the form, include a handwritten line that says, "This covers all aspects of a home inspection except the following..." If the inspector routinely leaves certain things for other professionals, it would be good if you knew that before you sign on the dotted line.

Arrange your schedule so you can be present during the inspection. Stay out of the way, but make notes about questions you have or observations that can help you later. If you notice something that looks suspicious, but it escapes the attention of the inspector, point it out immediately. At the end of the inspection, discuss any issues that seem important to you. When you receive the written report, check it against your notes. Sometimes things might have been omitted, and it's best to catch those mistakes early.

Chapter 19:

Clearing Contingencies

Chapter 17, "Preparing an Offer," mentioned several types of common real estate contingencies, such as the ability to cancel the contract if you can't obtain financing. Usually, you will have time limits within which to notify the seller that you've *cleared the contingencies* and will go forward with closing. In the alternative, you can inform the seller that you are cancelling the contract because of the failure of some contingency. You may then walk away or make another offer for less money. Whatever you do, you have to keep track of the contract terms and time limits.

- ☑ Identify all contract contingencies and deadlines
- ☑ Note which ones depend on other people
- ☑ Make a schedule of reminders and deadlines
- ☑ Put everything in writing
- ☑ Send the right notices

☑ Identify all contract contingencies and deadlines

Reread your contract in its entirety. If the seller used a preprinted form, it probably has different contingency provisions scattered across several paragraphs. Maybe none of them have deadlines, but another paragraph entirely will impose an overall time limit. It's boring stuff, but you'll have to read every single word of the contract if you want to make sure things get done on time.

Most often, you'll have a week or ten days during which to give the seller a signed commitment letter from some lender. If worded in that manner, the seller can cancel the contract if you don't deliver the letter on time—*even if you have a loan commitment*. Sometimes, the language will simply reference some sort of vague "financing contingency" that gives you the power to back out of the deal.

☑ Note which ones depend on other people

You'll need to hire a home inspector, work closely with a mortgage broker or loan officer, order a survey of rural property, and perform other such chores. This is not the time to start shopping—you should have already picked out your professionals well before contract-signing time. Make a list of everyone who must do something before closing can take place and all their contact information, especially email addresses and cell phone numbers. Most of them rarely spend any time in the office, so it's pointless to have only office telephone numbers.

☑ Make a schedule of reminders and deadlines

Buy or print out a calendar to be used solely for tracking your real estate closing. If purchasing one, try to get the wall-sized laminated type that lets you write things and easily erase them as needed. Mark all deadlines in red ink. Also note estimated completion dates given to you by the home inspector and other professionals hired by you. Don't let anyone off the hook with something as vague as, "I'll get it done as soon as possible."

Two days before any promised completion dates, call the person to check progress. You'll say, "I know your scheduled due date is two days from now. I was just calling to see if there's anything you need from me in order to finish on time." This is a gentle reminder to get busy, if they haven't already started. It also communicates the clear message that you're a person who pays attention to deadlines and finds them important.

The day your work is due, call and ask if you can pick up the completed product at their office the next day. If you have a deadline rapidly approaching and you can't personally retrieve whatever you need, agree to pay the extra money for overnight or messenger service. This is not the time to take chances on timely mail delivery.

☑ Put everything in writing

You should already have written contracts with all third parties. Any conversations about progress or additional information needed should be written on your real estate closing calendar. If using a computer calendar program, you may need to print a separate page for each day, so you'll have enough room for notes. Anything that varies the terms of your service contract, such as changing the completion date of a survey, should be confirmed in a letter or email to the provider.

It's especially important that all revisions to the real estate contract be put in writing and signed by all parties, just like the original agreement. Many unfortunate buyers have "worked with" sellers to extend closing deadlines time and again, with nothing in writing. All seemed friendly and cooperative until another buyer happened on the scene. That's when the original buyer was informed that he or she was in default, the earnest money would be retained, and the property sold to someone else.

☑ Send the right notices

As you lay each contingency to rest so it's no longer an issue that will prevent closing, write or email the seller or his or her real estate agent to let him or her know. You should do this even if the contract doesn't require it. It's only common courtesy, the seller is probably anxious, and he or she may have a purchase contract contingent on you buying his or her home. Your notices will cut down on the seller's anxiety. It's also likely the seller will be more willing to be flexible in case you need an extension on the closing date, because he or she will have evidence that you really are trying to get everything done on time.

Critical notices, such as notice that you are cancelling the contract because of the failure of a contingency, should be in writing and sent in the manner specified in the contract. You can send it more than one way, but at least follow the contract instructions. For example, there is usually a paragraph near the end of form contracts that discusses notices. It might say, "All notices under this contract are effective when mailed if sent by certified mail, or when transmitted if sent by fax...." So, a certified letter is timely when mailed, even if the post office loses it or the seller is out of town for a month when it's delivered. With regular mail or overnight delivery service, no one knows when the notice is effective, because the contract is silent on that point.

The seller will be upset that you are not proceeding with closing. You should take care of all the technical details properly so the seller can't keep your earnest money.

Chapter 20:
Seller Financing

A seller will often act as your lender in two situations. First is when he or she has a difficult or over-priced property. Holding the financing, usually at 2% less than a mortgage company would charge, can help a sale go through. If you buy a house under those circumstances, be sure to think about your plans. If you will sell or refinance in the next several years, you might owe more than the house is truly worth.

A seller will also hold the financing when it is a good investment decision for him or her. If the seller does not need the money to use for the purchase of another home, he or she may decide that a mortgage will earn a better return than CDs and be a safer investment than stock.

- ☑ Put important terms in the real estate contract
- ☑ Include a contract contingency for loan document review
- ☑ Offer to write the note and the mortgage
- ☑ Deliver the note and mortgage to the closing company

☑ Put important terms in the real estate contract

Almost all agreements related to real estate must be in writing. There are certain rare and very technical exceptions, but they come up only when someone forgets to put things in writing and then has to figure out a loophole to make the oral real estate contract enforceable. Don't get caught in that boat! In order for a seller financing agreement to be enforceable, the writing must contain these important terms:

☑ amount of the loan;

☑ interest rate;

☑ term of the loan;

☑ frequency of payments; and,

☑ names of the parties.

All other terms—such as late charges, grace periods, and insurance requirements—can be negotiated later.

If you and the seller cannot agree on those *secondary terms*, a court will decide what's reasonable under the circumstances. Leaving out one of the important terms from your contract will result in a court finding that the agreement is unenforceable.

Adjustable rate loans are a little bit tricky. Put the initial rate in the original contract, the frequency the rate can increase or decrease (once a year, for example), and the maximum interest rate possible, no matter what's happening in the marketplace. If you're comfortable specifying an index—the reference for calculating the interest, such as the one-year Treasury bill rate—then do so. Otherwise, the index rate can probably wait until the drafting of the final note and mortgage.

For more information, go to **www.wikipedia.com** and search for "adjustable rate mortgage."

☑ Include a contract contingency for loan document review

The worst thing you can do is have a short deadline for closing, such as thirty days, and spend the whole time haggling over details of the note and mortgage. When day thirty comes and goes, you'll be in default and the seller could cancel the contract.

Avoid that problem by including a contingency such as the following.

Buyer and Seller will have twenty-one days after contract signing to agree on the exact wording of the note and security documents to be executed at closing. If they are unable to agree by that time, Buyer may extend the closing date an additional twenty-one days in order to secure third-party financing, or Buyer may cancel the contract and receive a refund of the earnest money, or the parties may negotiate for an extension of the closing date, but with all other contract terms and conditions the same.

☑ Offer to write the note and the mortgage

Bear in mind, some states use mortgages and some use deeds of trust. There are slight differences between the two, but what you need to understand is that both give the lender security in real estate. In this book, the term *mortgage* will be used to describe both types of instruments.

If you have someone draft the loan documents, you are more likely to get borrower-friendly terms than if you let the seller write them. This is not to say your note and mortgage will leave the seller unprotected. It's a matter of perspective. For example, a seller's note might say you will be in default if you don't provide proof of insurance on the property. That's a common clause. What if you have insurance the whole time, but simply forget to provide proof to the seller? Are you in default? Technically, yes, and the seller could foreclose. Instead, your lawyer might have written that section to say, "Upon written request by seller, buyer will provide proof of insurance within a reasonable time afterwards, not to exceed ten days."

There are hundreds of similar things in the financing documents. Sure, everyone is on good terms and happy today, but that could change tomorrow. Make sure you are reasonably well protected.

Many times, the seller will want to write the note and mortgage. This is the most prudent thing for the seller, because he or she has all the risk. Don't argue, but do make sure you have your own attorney review and suggest changes. Remember, your attorney should be someone with experience in lending law.

☑ Deliver the note and mortgage to the closing company

The closing company, escrow company, or title attorney will need the note and mortgage as soon as possible before closing. They'll have to review the documents to make sure all requirements are met at closing and all the proper signatures obtained. The title insurance company will have to satisfy itself that there's nothing objectionable in the documents that could increase its risk for some reason. In addition, most jurisdictions charge a per-page fee for recording mortgages. No one can calculate the recording fees for the closing expenses until they know how long the mortgage document is.

Chapter 21:

Cancelling a Contract

Sadly, under some circumstances, you'll need to cancel a real estate contract. A surprising number of people think they can simply cancel or break a contract without consequences. That's not true. You'll need to read the agreement and make sure you are cancelling for a reason that's permitted. If you've changed your mind about buying, you may suffer more than the loss of your earnest money. Legally, you are liable for damages for breach of contract. The damages might be the difference between your contract price and what the seller is ultimately able to obtain, or it could be much more. If you knew the seller was relying on your closing to fund his or her own purchase of another home, you might be liable for the loss of the seller's new home because of his or her inability to close.

- ☑ Identify the contractual reason you are cancelling the contract
- ☑ Confirm the time limits within which you must give notice
- ☑ Make sure notice is given in the proper manner
- ☑ Obtain confirmation of the cancellation
- ☑ Obtain refund of earnest money

☑ Identify the contractual reason you are cancelling the contract

Review the contract to make sure you are cancelling for an allowable reason. This is a fail-safe step. It forces you to revisit the contract and track the exact language. Make a note of the section and paragraph so you can copy it into your notice letter.

If your particular reason is not one of the allowed ones, check the earnest money paragraph and the damages paragraphs. Do they limit your liability to loss of the earnest money and nothing more? You may be unhappy over losing that money, but it's far better than getting sued, hiring a lawyer, and possibly suffering a large judgment. In an area where the average legal fees are $150 per hour, it will usually take a minimum of $5,000 in legal fees to defend a simple breach of contract case. With extensive depositions and a jury trial, you could easily see that figure rise to $30,000 or more.

☑ Confirm the time limits within which you must give notice

No explanation is necessary as to why you should confirm the time limits in which you must give notice. You don't want to miss any deadlines.

☑ Make sure notice is given in the proper manner

If the contact says notice is effective when mailed by certified mail, then use certified mail. Don't reason that overnight delivery would be even better, because it's faster. If the contract is silent about delivery, then notice might not be effective until actually received by the seller. What if the seller is on vacation or has already moved?

You can—and should—send notices by multiple methods, as long as at least one of them is a type spelled out in the contract. Certified mail can be slow, so an email, fax, or overnight delivery copy would be fair to the seller, who might have to cancel his or her own purchase contract or take some other action.

Resist the urge to go into long explanations in writing, especially if you're angry or disappointed. Sometimes, these things can come back to bite you later. Be polite, but stick to the exact language of the contract when giving your reason for cancelling.

☑ Obtain confirmation of the cancellation

Ask the seller to sign the bottom of your notice confirming his or her recognition that the contract has been cancelled. Request that he or she fax or scan and email it back to you, or provide him or her with a prepaid overnight delivery envelope to return the confirmation to you. Many times, sellers will agree to a cancellation and only later discuss things with a lawyer, who might convince them to fight it. You can stop this sort of flip-flop by getting written confirmation right away. It also acts as an early warning for you—if the seller refuses to confirm, you know there's probably a fight coming your way. Finally, the company holding the earnest money usually requires the seller's consent before it will refund the money to you. Taking charge of securing the written confirmation will allow you to speed the process along.

☑ Obtain refund of earnest money

Send a letter to the company holding the earnest money. Reference your name, the seller's name, and the amount of the earnest money being held. Include a copy of your cancellation letter and a copy of the contract. If you have it, also send the seller's written confirmation of cancellation. Ask for a refund of the earnest money and a phone call advising you of the date and time when you can pick up the check. Don't rely on the check being dropped in the mail. If you can't make it to the offices, ask for overnight delivery or wire transfer. You will usually have to pay a fee, but it's minimal.

Section V:
Closing

Chapter 22:

Deciding How You Want to Hold Title

Most closing companies assume that a husband and wife will hold title as joint tenants with right of survivorship. In other words, when the first one dies, the survivor automatically has the whole property without going through probate. Closing companies assume that all other co-purchasers will be tenants in common. There may be many reasons why you want to do something different. If the deed is silent about how title will be held, different states have different rules about how to interpret the deed. In most states, the law will say it's supposed to be a tenancy in common.

This chapter discusses the most common ways to hold title, and the pros and cons of each.

- ☑ Sole ownership in one person's name
- ☑ Tenants in common
- ☑ Joint tenants with right of survivorship
- ☑ Tenancy by the entireties
- ☑ Limited liability company
- ☑ Ask the title company about other ways to hold real estate

☑ Sole ownership in one person's name

Even when married, one spouse will often take title to the home in his or her own name. This may be for estate planning purposes, or problems with ex-spouses or other creditors. It might be because the buyers are mature and with substantial other assets, but one or the other provided all the money to purchase the home. In a community property state, the non-title holder will still have rights in the property if there's a divorce. Non-community property states sometimes give widows and widowers limited rights in property held by their deceased spouse. In the event of divorce, a judge can transfer ownership involuntarily.

NOTE: *Different ways of owning real estate have names that include the word "tenants" or "tenancy." This has nothing to do with landlords and rentals. The words are a result of legal concepts we inherited from England, when no one could truly own land except the King. All others were simply "tenants," even if many generations of heirs could inherit the "tenancy."*

☑ Tenants in common

With tenancy in common, two or more owners have specific percentages of ownership, which don't have to be equal. Each can sell his or her percentage to someone else. If one dies, that share goes according to his or her will or the laws of *intestate succession*—statutes that determine who gets what if there's no will. If the monetary limits in your state are met, the property must go through probate. A divorce judge can transfer ownership, and creditors of one party can seize that party's share and force a sale of the property. This is a common ownership style for partners in second marriages, each with children and substantial other assets. It is also common with nonmarital partners.

☑ Joint tenants with right of survivorship

In a joint tenancy with right of survivorship, two or more owners share ownership in equal amounts. If one owner dies, his or her rights to the property die also, so the final survivor gets everything, without going through probate. However, there may be estate taxes. One owner can sell his or her share before death, but there are tricky consequences. At the very least, the new owner will not have survivorship rights. Consult a lawyer in your state for the rules. In case of a divorce or other legal battle, a judge can make orders transferring ownership, and a creditor of one party can seize that share and force a sale of the property. This is a common ownership style for husbands and wives, or parents and their adult children.

☑ Tenancy by the entireties

Tenancy by the entireties is recognized by some states as a special way for husbands and wives to hold title to real estate. It's currently limited to spouses, but all the same-sex relationship litigation may change this in the future. The ownership is identical to a joint tenancy with right of survivorship, *except* that it can't be destroyed. One partner cannot transfer his or her share and convert the ownership to a tenancy in common. A creditor of only one spouse can't execute on the property. Usually, a divorce judge cannot make orders transferring ownership. This is all good if you want to protect the marital home from creditors. It's bad if you ever end up in divorce court, because it will force you to agree on who gets the home (and by that time, there's usually very little the parties can agree on).

☑ Limited liability company

The limited liability company is almost always an estate planning tool for extremely valuable properties. It's complicated and has to be done exactly right. If you think you might be interested, consult with a legal or financial professional.

Beware, because these professionals sometimes have tunnel vision about the all the terrific aspects of this device and overlook some of the drawbacks. In Florida, for example, individuals are protected from real estate taxes increasing too rapidly. People can file for a homestead exemption if they live full-time on their property. With a homestead exemption, the tax assessor's appraisal of your property can increase only a certain percentage each year. That means your taxes can increase only a small amount each year. If homes around you are selling in the millions, but you bought yours many years ago for $75,000, your taxes are going to be dramatically less than the neighbors.

Taking title in the name of a limited liability company prevents you from obtaining the homestead exemption. Also, insurance might be more expensive and tax deductions may be smaller. Be sure to examine the complete financial picture before choosing this type of ownership.

☑ Ask the title company about other ways to hold real estate

There could be any number of strange variations in state laws. Alabama has something called a *tenancy in common with cross contingent remainders*. It's virtually identical to the tenancy by the entireties, except you don't have to be married to take advantage of it. If you have unusual needs not met by traditional property ownership, do some research to see if something else might be available.

Chapter 23:
Information to Give the Title or Escrow Company

Usually, a real estate agent or mortgage broker will take care of the closing details for you, or at least assist in their completion. Sometimes you may need to take this responsibility for yourself. The more information the closing company has, the more efficiently it can work towards a speedy conclusion to the purchase. Last-minute surprises cause delays and can cost you extra money due to increased interest rates, overnight package delivery charges, and possibly attorney's fees. Most of the following items don't require an explanation. They either ensure the deed is drawn correctly, the loan documents are accurate, the money is distributed properly, or nothing causes delays in issuing title insurance, such as unforeseen liens or questions about identity.

You should also ask the previous owner for information on items that will make living in your new home much easier.

☑ **Title or escrow company**
☑ **Prior owner**

☑ Title or escrow company

The following items are what the closing company will need. If other people have to supply some things, such as the seller's Social Security number, stay on top of them and make sure it happens on time.

- ☑ Copy of the purchase contract
- ☑ Recent tax bills for the property
- ☑ A copy of the seller's deed, if available
- ☑ If possible, a copy of the seller's title insurance from his or her own purchase (this could save you money)
- ☑ Information regarding how the purchasers will hold title
- ☑ Full names, addresses, and Social Security numbers of purchasers
- ☑ Full names, addresses, and Social Security numbers of sellers
- ☑ Name and contact information for any homeowners association
- ☑ Name and contact information for condo association or co-op board
- ☑ Name and contact information for buyer's lender
- ☑ Copy of lender's estimated closing statement
- ☑ Name and contact information for seller's mortgage company
- ☑ Name and contact information for anyone else who will be paid from proceeds, such as an IRS lien, former spouse, second mortgage, etc.
- ☑ Names and contact information for all people hired to complete reports before closing can take place—inspectors, surveyors, appraisers, wood infestation reports, and anything else
- ☑ Names and contact information for real estate agents who will be paid at closing

Ask of there's anything else they might need, and add it to your list. You should call again, about a week before closing, just to make sure everything's on track and there are no new requirements.

How it works in the real world: Title Insurance

All lenders will require that you obtain mortgagee's title insurance at closing. (The lender is called the mortgagee. The borrower is called the mortgagor.) This protects them in case there is a defect in the seller's title. Examples could be an IRS lien that was overlooked, the failure to obtain all necessary signatures on a deed, or even outright fraud if the seller already sold the property to someone else. You'll need to specify that you also want owner's coverage. The premium increase is usually very small. Without it, suppose the IRS seizes your home because of back taxes owed by the seller. The title insurance company will pay your lender the amount of the loan balance. You will get nothing, even though you may have substantial equity in the property. Also, think about buying title insurance in an amount greater than the purchase price, especially if you are renovating a property—it could be worth substantially more than the original sales amount.

☑ Prior owner

There are many things the seller would be happy to share with you, if only you think to ask. All of the following suggestions will help you save money, time, trouble, and your dignity.

- ☑ Appliance manuals
- ☑ Warranty information
- ☑ Location of circuit breakers
- ☑ Location of main power cutoff for the house
- ☑ Location of main gas line cutoff for the house
- ☑ Location of main water cutoff for the entire house, in case of broken pipes
- ☑ Information regarding what all the switches control
- ☑ Location of the water heater
- ☑ Instructions on how to relight the pilot light on a gas water heater
- ☑ Zoning for multiple water heaters
- ☑ If multiple HVAC units, which thermostats control what areas
- ☑ Instructions regarding multiple phone lines and jack locations
- ☑ Location of the septic tank and field lines
- ☑ Location of any sewer line clean-outs
- ☑ Location of sprinkler system controls and how to operate
- ☑ Information regarding anything quirky, such as secret panels
- ☑ Contact information for trusted repair people
- ☑ Instructions regarding routine preventive measures
- ☑ Recommendations for lawn care, pool maintenance, and security monitoring
- ☑ Instructions regarding landscape plants requiring special care
- ☑ Information about neighborhood etiquette, such as leaf blowing before 9 a.m.
- ☑ Contact information for reliable baby-sitters

☑ Names of baby-sitters and repair people to avoid at all costs

☑ Contact information for reputable cleaning assistance

☑ The name of the best pizza delivery company and the size of an acceptable tip

☑ Estimate of the time of day the mail is delivered

☑ Address of the post office servicing the home

☑ Location of the place to vote for the district

☑ Location of nearest emergency medical care

☑ Day and approximate time of trash pickup

☑ Any sorting or recycling rules for trash pickup

☑ Any special cleaning recommendations, such as for hardwood floors

☑ Names and addresses of possible friends for your children

☑ Any general advice the seller wants to volunteer

Chapter 24:
Finalizing Loan Arrangements

You'll need to closely monitor the loan process to make sure nothing causes any delays or surprises, or increases the amount of money you must bring to the closing table.

- ☑ Send out new requests for proposal
- ☑ Fill out an application and secure a written commitment
- ☑ Determine the expiration of any interest rate lock
- ☑ Complete loan-related requirements
- ☑ Obtain an estimated closing statement from the lender
- ☑ Make sure loan package and requirements are sent to the closing company

☑ Send out new requests for proposal

Chapter 3, "Shopping for Financing," explains the process of obtaining competitive quotes for your mortgage loan using *requests for proposals* (RFPs). Fairly early in your shopping process, you should narrow the field of potential lenders down to about three. Once you have a signed contract to purchase a particular property, revisit the quotes from the top three mortgage sources. If your anticipated purchase price was roughly equal to the actual contract price, and if your credit score or financial conditions have not changed significantly, then choose the top three prospects. Dramatic changes in finances or purchase price should prompt you to start the RFP process all over again, but you'll need to move quickly.

☑ Fill out an application and secure a written commitment

Contact the top three contenders and give them a copy of their old quote and your purchase contract, and complete a formal loan application. Common wisdom says multiple credit inquiries will reduce your credit score. This isn't exactly true; they all count as one inquiry if they come within a very short period of time, usually two weeks. This simply indicates you are shopping for the best deal. In addition, credit inquiries within the last thirty days don't affect your current score at all.

When the quotes come back, don't be afraid to negotiate. Reread Chapter 3, "Shopping for Financing," so you are aware of some of the expenses that can be waived. Ask the loan officer or mortgage broker to give you an example of the savings with discount points. If necessary, let them all see each other's offers and ask if they can do better. You could save thousands of dollars in interest and closing costs. When you make a final decision, obtain a written loan commitment letter. The words "subject to underwriting" mean you don't have a loan commitment, you have an offer to extend financing if the lender wants to. The only contingencies in a loan commitment on a home should be satisfactory appraisal, termite and home inspection, paid homeowner's insurance for one year, and acceptable title insurance.

☑ Determine the expiration of any interest rate lock

Your lender may guarantee a certain interest rate for a particular number of days. Make sure this comes from the actual lender, not from a mortgage broker. There are many abuses in this regard, with people paying for interest rate locks but not receiving them. When that happens, it's because the mortgage broker is acting fraudulently and gambling that interest rates won't rise within the time period. He or she keeps your money instead of paying it to the lender to secure a lock. Make a note of the expiration date for any rate locks. You'll need to work against that deadline in making sure closing takes place on time.

☑ Complete loan-related requirements

Many first-time buyers wait until the last minute to purchase insurance. They just don't think about it until the closing company calls, at the last minute, to obtain proof of insurance. If you identify all loan requirements early, you'll be able to work on them in a timely manner and avoid making costly last-minute mistakes.

Your lender will hire the appraiser. Request that the report be completed one week before closing. Your loan will be based on the appraised value, not the purchase price. If the value is lower than the contract price, you'll need time to come up with a larger down payment; negotiate a price reduction with the seller; or, convince the appraiser the property is worth more because of comparable sales or additional features the appraiser might have overlooked.

☑ Obtain an estimated closing statement from the lender

A good faith estimate can be wildly off base, but at least it's a start. It will show only the estimated loan-related expenses, so it won't give you a complete picture. If you request one, the closing company must provide you with an estimated closing statement at least twenty-four hours before closing, showing all expenses and distributions.

☑ Make sure loan package and requirements are sent to the closing company

Usually, the loan package and other requirements for closing all come together without your assistance. It's a good idea to check on progress, though, in case your help is necessary. About a week before closing, call the closing company to see if it has received everything it needs from your lender. If so, it will include a checklist of items that must be completed before the lender will fund the mortgage. Ask for a copy of the checklist so you can assist with building fires under anyone who needs it. Remember, you and the seller are the two people most interested in having closing take place on time. Everyone else has a thousand other pressures in their lives, and you might not be number one.

If the closing company does not yet have a loan package, call your lender or broker to find out the problem. Most mistakes are caused by last minute rushes on closings. Many things can go wrong at the last minute. The best solution is to make sure there's no frantic activity on the day of closing.

Chapter 25:
Closing

Closing day is an exhilarating event. The process is rather boring, but you can turn it into the joyous celebration it should be. The trick is to be prepared.

- ☑ Make sure you have all documents necessary for closing
- ☑ Find out if you must bring certified funds
- ☑ Be prepared to ask questions
- ☑ Use this opportunity to obtain free advice

☑ Make sure you have all documents necessary for closing

If in doubt about whether you have all documents necessary for closing, call the closing company and ask them what you should bring. Usually, it will have everything already, but there might be exceptions, such as proof of insurance or something similar.

NOTE: *You will probably need to bring a current, government-issued ID for identification purposes. A driver's license usually is all you need, but verify this with the closing company.*

☑ Find out if you must bring certified funds

Most closing companies require certified funds, but some in small communities will accept personal checks. They won't give you the deed before the check clears the bank, but at least you'll have the semblance of trust. The need to obtain certified funds usually works in your favor, because it forces everyone to calculate the final closing numbers in time for you to obtain a bank check.

☑ Be prepared to ask questions

This is your closing. Everyone else will be bored silly, will know exactly what all the documents mean, and will want to rush through signatures. Slow down the pace. You're the buyer, the one bringing the money to the table. That puts you in control. Don't sign anything unless you thoroughly understand what it is. Ask for explanations and take time to read documents you think deserve closer scrutiny.

☑ Use this opportunity to obtain free advice

You have a wonderful opportunity to obtain free advice on a great variety of real estate-related topics. Use this time wisely to find out answers to the following questions.

- ☑ How will my deed and mortgage be recorded?
- ☑ What do I need to do regarding real estate or school taxes?
- ☑ What local tax exemptions should I apply for, and how do I do it?
- ☑ Did any of the expenses on this closing seem unusually high or low?
- ☑ Can I do anything differently next time to save time or money?

Chapter 26:

Document Management

You will have a large stack of documents to sign at closing. The details will vary, depending on your state, particular lender requirements, and whether there is any government involvement such as with a VA loan. Whoever is doing the closing will have a list of all documents necessary for your loan.

- ☑ **Obtain a list of closing documents**
- ☑ **Request multiple copies of important paperwork**
- ☑ **File papers someplace you can find them again**

☑ Obtain a list of closing documents

All closing companies and attorneys work with checklists. It's the only way to complete a transaction as quickly and efficiently as possible. They will know all the paperwork necessary for a typical sale. Your lender will supply the closing company with a list of its loan documents. Sometime before closing, obtain these lists. At closing, you want to make sure that you have copies of everything on the list.

☑ Request multiple copies of important paperwork

At the end of closing, you will be presented with a set of all documents related to your portion of the transaction. Some documents, such as the seller's copy of the HUD-1 Settlement Sheet, may not be given to you. That is because some information may be private. For example, if the seller had a tax lien or unpaid child support that was paid out of closing proceeds, he or she might not care to have you know that information. Details regarding distribution of sale proceeds might be spelled out on the Seller's HUD-1, but not on yours.

Take the time to make sure you have all important documents. You should also obtain extra copies of some of them. This is most easily done at the closing company, rather than later at an office supply or copy store.

At the very least, you can expect to receive the following documents:

> ☑ *Deed.* Usually, the closing company will retain the original deed and deliver it to the appropriate authorities for filing in the public records. After it is scanned or copied, as the case may be, the original will be mailed to you. Upon receipt, you will need to take it to the tax assessor's office in order to declare any homestead or other exemptions to which you might be entitled. At the closing, ask for two

extra copies of the deed. Some school systems and utilities may require a copy.

☑ *Promissory note.* This is your agreement to repay the lender. The mortgage company keeps the original note and will return it to you when it has been paid in full. At closing, ask for one extra copy. You should place this copy in your tax files for the current year. In case you do not receive your interest-paid statement at the end of the year, you or your tax preparer will be able to calculate the interest deduction from the promissory note.

☑ *Mortgage or Deed of Trust.* This documents gives the lender a security interest in the property you are buying, so it can foreclose if you don't make your payments. The closing company will retain the original mortgage in order to deliver it to the proper authorities for recordation, usually the county courthouse. Afterwards, the original will be returned to your lender for retention until the loan has been paid in full. At that time, the lender will execute new documents showing that the lien has been extinguished. It will send the original mortgage to you. Ask for one extra copy of this document so you can give it to your insurance agent. Usually, lender requirements regarding insurance are spelled out in the mortgage, not in the promissory note.

☑ *Truth in Lending Disclosure.* This document is signed by you as acknowledgment that you've been informed of the annual percentage rate, total payments over the lifetime of the loan, and other such matters. Federal law requires these disclosures. You do not need extra copies for any reason.

☑ *HUD-1 Settlement Statement.* This is an accounting of all sums changing hands at closing, and the fees and expenses charged to each side. It's called a HUD-1 because the Department of Housing and Urban

Development requires its use on all consumer loans. Their form number is HUD-1, so the name has stuck. Ask for three extra copies. You will need one to stay with your important documents for this year's tax return, one to be given to your tax preparer, and one to put in the file for next year's taxes. (Some closing items must be deducted over several years. Putting a copy of the HUD-1 in each new year's tax file will remind you of this.)

☑ *Lender's escrow agreement.* If a portion of each month's payment will include sums for taxes and insurance, you will need to sign an escrow agreement with the lender. It allows them to collect money from you, and hold it for your benefit for payment in the future of taxes and insurance.

☑ *Non-foreign affidavit required under Section 1445 of the Internal Revenue Code.* Because of the Foreign Investment in Real Property Tax Act, if the seller is a nonresident alien, some portion of the sale proceeds might have to be withheld by the closing company. This is in case the seller does not pay all taxes due on the transaction; it's similar to payroll withholding. The affidavit, saying the seller does not fall under the law, solves the withholding problem.

☑ *Mechanics' and Materialmen's (M&M) Lien.* This affidavit is usually signed by the seller. It says that no work has been done on the property within the prior statutory period, usually six months, so that no one is entitled to file an M&M lien for unpaid work. In the alternative, the affidavit might say that all work has been paid in full, and if that turns out to be incorrect, the seller will reimburse the title company for any sums it must pay to clear up liens.

☑ *Affidavit or certificate of occupancy.* In this document, you state under oath that you will reside in the property. This is because investors do not qualify for some mortgage loan programs, which are available only for persons who will occupy the property they are buying.

There may be other documents depending on particular requirements of your state law and your individual transaction. Do not leave the closing company offices until you are sure you have copies of everything and you understand the purpose of all documents. Keep everything in a safe place, where they can be easily found in case of need.

☑ File papers someplace you can find them again

You will need to refer back to your closing file a surprising number of times. Be sure to put your copies with other important papers, such as your wills, insurance policies, and car titles. If you need to make copies, take out the entire file, not just the single piece of paper you need. Often, individual sheets of paper get lost in the shuffle, and we sometimes forget to return them to their proper place. An entire file folder filled with documents is harder to overlook.

Section VI:
Moving

Chapter 27:
Preparing to Leave Your Rental Property

In all the excitement of looking forward to your new home, don't forget about wrapping things up at your old place. Also, home shoppers with insufficient public credit information can sometimes use their landlords as credit references. You want to make sure you keep a good payment history there. Here are some things to think about as you prepare to say good-bye to your rental property.

- ☑ Read your current lease
- ☑ Start a change of address box
- ☑ Make a list of all deposits and when they will be refunded
- ☑ Get rid of stuff BEFORE the move
- ☑ Ask if your landlord offers incentives if you find a replacement tenant
- ☑ Schedule a landlord walk-through inspection

☑ Read your current lease

Up to now, you may have been interested only in the amount of the monthly rent check. Suddenly, though, it's important to know exact lease ending dates, if there is an automatic renewal clause, deadlines for notices, the precise requirements for moving out, and the timing and circumstances of security deposit refunds. All of this will be spelled out in your lease.

Although your rent is due on the first of each month, the lease ending date might be mid-month. This could cause important changes in your planning for a closing date on a purchase. Talk early with your landlord about your ability to extend the lease on a month-to-month basis if that should prove necessary, and the rental rate for that concession. Some charge a higher rent for short-term leases. Beware that failure to give the required notice, sometimes as early as ninety days before the lease ends, could result in automatic renewal for another year. You suffer more than the loss of your deposit if you break a lease or default on your obligations. The landlord can sue you, and garnish wages or file a lien against your new home.

Many tenants assume they've paid the last month's rent in advance, when in reality, they paid a security/cleaning deposit. Based on their incorrect beliefs, they don't pay the last month's rent, and then suffer late fees and a deteriorated relationship with their landlord. Reading your lease will avoid these problems.

Budgeting for every penny will become important when you approach the closing table with all its expenses and consider the cost of moving. Make sure you know about any move-out fees at your current home. Many apartment projects or condo rental properties impose a move-out impact fee to compensate for the additional wear and tear on hallways, carpeting, elevators, and other such common areas.

Moving trucks may be prohibited on certain days or hours. You might need to schedule use of a freight elevator, so you aren't competing with other people trying to move in or out.

Finally, check for the timing and prerequisites for your security deposit refund. Some companies hold deposits for as long as forty-five days in order to give themselves time to inspect and evaluate repairs or cleaning. Many require a valid forwarding address, just in case they need to contact you afterwards. There may be other surprises waiting in your lease. Things that didn't seem important when you moved in might be critical now.

☑ Start a change of address box

Get any kind of container and start dropping things in it to remind you about address changes. You'll find this easier than if you begin a list or journal—the easier the task, the more likely it will be done well.

What goes in the box? At a minimum you will want the following.

- ☑ One copy of each magazine you subscribe to
- ☑ One copy of each catalog you want waiting at your new home
- ☑ So-called "junk mail" you secretly enjoy receiving
- ☑ Christmas cards
- ☑ Wedding announcements
- ☑ Doctors' bills and insurance claim reports
- ☑ Warranty notices
- ☑ Bank statements
- ☑ Retirement plans
- ☑ Civic and church group information
- ☑ Medical, dental, and veterinary checkup reminders

Make notes about organizations with infrequent mailings, such as alumni associations that might want to find you for a reunion. Once you know your new address, it's a simple matter to go through the box and send out the appropriate notices.

☑ Make a list of all deposits and when they will be refunded

It's surprisingly easy to forget about some of your security deposits in all the rush and excitement of a new home. Many months later you might remember, and then it will be hard work to find out why you didn't receive a refund. Making a list of the names, phone numbers, and account numbers for all deposits will help you keep track of them easily. Typically, you'll have deposits with your landlord, all utilities, some self-storage facilities, some mail-handling services, and some parking garages. Find out their policies for refunds. In addition, ask all utility companies about waiver of deposits at your new home if you have a good payment record with them.

☑ Get rid of stuff BEFORE the move

Everyone's done it—in the last-minute frenzy of packing for a move, you start throwing things in boxes. No time to sort, no time to evaluate whether to keep or not. As a result, a lot of time and money is wasted moving junk, only to throw it away as you unpack. Avoid the rush and start early. Resolve to clean out one drawer or cabinet per weekday, one closet per weekend. All those clothes you think might fit again some day? Get rid of them, or go ahead and pack them now and get them out of the way. The same thing goes for anything else you think *might* be useful in the future. If you're not using it now, discard it or pack it.

☑ Ask if your landlord offers incentives if you find a replacement tenant

Under most state laws, a landlord cannot pay a commission to anyone except a licensed real estate agent or their own employees for finding a replacement tenant. However, some states allow referral fees, gifts, or discounts if they are less than a certain amount, perhaps $50. Others permit specialized programs for existing tenants to receive concessions for referrals. Check with your landlord. Even if he or she cannot pay you, but will give a new tenant one month's free rent, you may be able to use that information to your advantage and help out a friend.

☑ Schedule a landlord walk-through inspection

Even if it's not a common practice in your community, insist that some representative of the landlord conduct an inspection immediately after you move out. Most leases allow *normal wear and tear* in a property without penalty, but your idea of normal wear and tear might be different from the landlord's. Large apartment communities usually have move-out inspection checklists for their managers. Ask if you can have a copy so you know what to do beforehand.

You might prefer to perform minor repairs and cleaning yourself, rather than suffer the loss of your security/cleaning deposit. Have a written statement of acceptance ready for the landlord's signature after the inspection. All you need is one sentence: "Landlord accepts the property in its current condition without any need for repairs or additional cleaning." At the end of the inspection, while everyone is still on the property, obtain the necessary signature. Don't wait until later, when memories dim or people rethink their opinions.

Chapter 28:
Moving

The closing is a big sigh of relief, but there's still a lot to be done. Hopefully, you've been working on moving-related items all along. Here's a master list for managing the physical move to your new home.

- ☑ As soon as you start looking for a new home
- ☑ When you know you want to make an offer on a home
- ☑ After your offer is accepted and before closing
- ☑ Moving day

☑ As soon as you start looking for a new home

- ☑ Create a moving box
- ☑ Start a list of anyone who will need to know your new address
- ☑ Set up a box for discards
- ☑ Interview movers or price moving truck rentals
- ☑ Find a source for inexpensive boxes
- ☑ Confirm the expiration date of your lease

☑ Create a moving box

Creating a *moving box* gets you started on the organization it will take to make sure everything goes smoothly. If you're not the organized type, don't stress—this is not some super-structured thing. All you need is a container in which you can file or simply toss things, depending on your personality. It doesn't matter if you stencil the words **MOVING BOX** on all four sides, top and bottom, or if it's your little secret that the laundry basket on the closet floor is your moving box. Its only purpose is to be handy, to be portable, and to hold all the important stuff you need as you get ready to move, plus all the critical things you'll want immediately after the move but before you unpack.

In the beginning, the moving box will probably hold just a few items—a folder with change of address forms (or a stack of magazine covers and old envelopes), information about movers, and maybe a copy of your current lease. If you have small children, let each one decorate his or her own box. It will help them feel like a part of the process, and will remove some anxiety. Right before the move, they'll place their very favorite toys, books, and clothes in their own personal boxes, for immediate access in your new home. On the big day, these special moving boxes will travel with you in your car, or will be the last things placed on the moving truck and the first things taken off.

☑ Start a list of anyone who will need to know your new address

Start collecting mailing labels from magazines and catalogs, as well as names and addresses of people who will need your new information after you move. Remember friends and relatives, including people you rarely hear from except for holidays, birthdays, weddings, and funerals. Doctors, pharmacists, veterinarians, accountants, and clergy will all send you mail, occasionally. Your old schools will want to keep track of you, for future reunion notices. Don't forget insurance companies, banks, auto lenders, school loans, and any employer who will need to send you a W-2 before the year ends, especially if you'll want it quickly so you can file for a refund. New car owners will want to receive warranty or recall information at their new homes.

☑ Set up box for discards

Most people pack at the last minute and end up flinging everything they own into boxes and then sorting it out afterwards. That's why you see huge piles of garbage at the curb of the new home *after* people move in! Every worthless thing you pack and then discard costs you time and money. That's why you should get a large cardboard box and start throwing into it those things you no longer want or need. Don't make a project out of it—simply go through one drawer a day, and then one cabinet shelf a day, one closet per weekend, and so on. Toss all the expendables into your discard box, where they'll go through a sort of cooling down period in case you change your mind. When the box is full, get rid of the contents, whether that means dumpster or charity. Resist the urge to save things for a garage sale unless you think you'll make more than $200; otherwise, your time is better spent doing something else.

☑ Interview movers or price moving truck rentals

Now is a good time to interview movers or obtain prices on moving trucks. Most will need to come to your home in order to give you an estimate. Interstate movers charge by the pound, while cross-town movers charge by the half day, with price depending on the size of the truck. There's an online service at **www.uship.com** that works like eBay, except for moving and shipping services. Be sure to confirm that any mover is insured, and find out the amount of covered losses and any deductible if your property is damaged or missing.

Check with your insurance agent about rental trucks—most car policies do not automatically cover moving trucks over a certain size. Find out what happens if you schedule a move, and on the morning of your move, the truck breaks down. You want to know the company has enough depth that the loss of one truck doesn't force you to reschedule everything. Write up complete notes regarding each likely candidate, and put those notes in your moving box so you can find them again easily.

☑ Find a source for inexpensive boxes

Boxes are expensive. Grocery and liquor store boxes usually have roaches hiding in them. On the other hand, copy shops, schools, and libraries often go through hundreds of really sturdy copy paper boxes with lids—they just don't have them all at once. See if you can stop by once a week or so and relieve them of their "trash"—you'll be a hero, I promise you. If that's not possible, there are several companies that sell bulk quantities of boxes at about half the price you'll find elsewhere. You'll need to plan ahead and allow enough time for shipment. Some good sources include **www.dial-a-box.com** (866-434-2522), **www.uline.com** (800-958-5463), and **www.packing.com** (954-455-8842). Wardrobe boxes, which include a bar on which to hang clothes, are a wonderful investment because everything won't be wrinkled afterwards, and they can be used for off-season clothing storage.

☑ Confirm the expiration date of your lease

Finally, if you're currently renting, get a copy of your lease and read it, beginning to end. You want to find out the expiration date. It might be different than you remembered. It's also important to discover any notices you must give in order to prevent the lease from renewing automatically, or any other notices or inspections necessary to obtain a full refund of your security deposit. This information must be factored into your timing as you search for, and make an offer on, a new home. Make an extra copy of the lease and put it in your moving box, so it's handy for future reference.

☑ When you know you want to make an offer on a home

☑ Check schedules for movers or price moving truck rentals
☑ Find out about self-storage availability
☑ Talk to an insurance agent about moving and storage insurance
☑ Obtain a firm quote if using professional movers

Well, now it's all starting to get real, isn't it? Reread your lease for the termination date and the timing of any required notices. If that checks out okay, then resist the urge to make an offer immediately, and find out a few moving-related things first.

☑ Check schedules for movers or price moving truck rentals

Did you know it's virtually impossible to rent a truck, or schedule a mover, for any three-day holiday weekend? That's because everyone else in the United States is also using that extra time to relocate. If that's when you want to move, then make confirmed reservations early, before you sign a real estate purchase contract saying you'll close on or before a certain date. Otherwise, just find out which dates are busier than others, so you can schedule accordingly—you might want to specify closing in forty-five days, rather than the typical thirty days. Bear in mind that many things can happen to delay a closing, so you'll need some contingency plans. Which movers can offer you some flexibility? Will your current landlord allow you to hold over for a few days or even weeks? Worst case—can you rent self-storage space in case you have to move twice?

Many professional movers require payment by certified funds before they will unload your possessions. Find out early how and when you will have to pay for the move. If there's a delay in closing, some will allow you to keep your belongings in their truck and pay a huge fee each day, but most won't do it for any amount of money. You'll need to off-load into storage and then arrange new movers for the home. If there's a loss or damage, most moving company insurers will fight with you over the details, and claim you can't prove they're the ones who ripped the doors off your china cabinet. If possible, invest in a digital camera and takes lots of photos before the move.

☑ Find out about self-storage availability

If closing is delayed, you may need to put everything in storage for a few days or weeks. Early education about the choices available in your market avoid panic and poor decisions if there are any surprises. Look for climate-controlled storage if your area is very hot, very cold, humid, or suffers wide temperature variations between day and night. If available, try to find a facility with individual door alarms, cameras that record to a computer rather than videotape, an underground storm sewer system rather than ditches in the middle of driveways, and professional pest control. All of these things will help with the safety of your possessions.

☑ Talk to an insurance agent about moving and storage insurance

Make sure you have full coverage while your goods are in transit or in storage. Usually there is no additional fee, but you must advise your insurance agent before the move regarding your coverage needs. A very few companies will not cover those risks at all. Find out early if yours is one of them, and plan accordingly by selecting another company or by purchasing separate insurance from the moving company and from the storage facility. Be aware that most storage insurance has a maximum coverage of $15,000 per unit.

☑ Obtain a firm quote if using professional movers

Get the hourly or per-pound rate in writing. Plus, be sure to obtain an estimate of the likely total charges.

☑ After your offer is accepted and before closing

  ☑ Arrange for utility service shut-offs and turn-ons
  ☑ Meet with an insurance agent for an insurance binder
  ☑ Confirm movers
  ☑ Schedule and conduct a walk-through with the sellers
  ☑ Make reservations for house cleaning assistance
  ☑ Find out the requirements at your children's new school and make sure everyone is familiar with the new neighborhood
  ☑ Prepare all change of address notices
  ☑ Send an introduction to your new neighbors
  ☑ Begin packing
  ☑ Buy colored tags and labels

This is the time period when you make all your appointments and schedule everything to come together at the right times.

☑ Arrange for utility service shut-offs and turn-ons

All utilities will need to be disconnected at your old residence and service started at the new one. Don't forget the little non-utility services that you depend on—things like newspapers, laundry pickup/delivery, and lawn care services if you currently rent a house. Set aside twenty minutes per phone call, because this always takes longer than you would think. Be sure to write down the names of everyone you speak to, and ask for confirmation numbers for your orders, in case the closing date changes and you have to revise utility disconnect dates. During this time, you should also find out if you need to move your trash carts or obtain new ones, and if you will move any satellite receivers or obtain new ones.

☑ Meet with an insurance agent for an insurance binder

Meet with your insurance agent to bind coverage on the new home, as of the date of closing. Find out if your household goods will be covered while they're in transit, and if any rental truck you drive will be covered under your regular auto policy. If there are any gaps, ask your agent what to do. Be sure to get two or three copies of a certificate of coverage or proof of insurance on the new home. Deliver one to the closing agent, and keep the extras in your moving box, just in case.

☑ Confirm movers

Make your final, confirmed reservations with firm quotes for moving truck and assistance, or professional movers. If planning on moving yourself, you can sometimes get help from moving company employees willing to work on the weekends or evenings. This is not unethical, and is encouraged by many long-distance moving companies as a way for their people to earn extra money. You might want to schedule a walk-through of the new home with a moving company representative. If there's something unusual (for example, steep stairs, narrow hallways with sharp corners) that will cause the price to increase, you need to know early.

☑ Schedule and conduct a walk-through with the sellers

After closing, you may never see the sellers again. They could move to another city, or you might feel reluctant about calling them with questions. Try to arrange a final meeting, at the home, before closing but after the sellers have moved out.

This is your opportunity to see anything formerly hidden by area rugs, furniture, or art work. Will repairs or cleaning be necessary? Under the contract, who will have to pay for repairs? In some circumstances, you may be able to cancel a contract if defects are serious. Your ability to do this will vary from state to state, and depending on the exact language of your contract.

☑ Make reservations for house cleaning assistance

If you think it will be necessary, schedule cleaning services and repair people to arrive before the moving truck.

Insider trick: Your New Home's Quirks

The walk-through is your final chance to learn everything quirky about your new home, before it becomes a problem. Ask the seller about the following items, plus anything else that occurs to you. Tape record the answers if possible rather than taking notes. Find out:

- ☑ Function of all light switches—what they control.
- ☑ Location of circuit breakers. See if the individual breakers are labeled or if you will need to do that. This is easiest before you move in.
- ☑ Location and instructions for sprinkler system controls, pool equipment, hvac, and/or security system.
- ☑ How to operate the self-cleaning oven, change the filters on the refrigerator or other water purification systems, use the whirlpool tub, spa or steam shower, and/or re-light the pilot light for heater or water heater.
- ☑ Unusual problems and how to fix them, such as "About twice a year the garbage disposal will quit working. Press the reset button, located here, and everything will be fine again."
- ☑ Location of attic and basement access, any storm shelters and any hidden rooms or safes.
- ☑ Location of cable, satellite and/or telephone line entrance into the home, and any wiring panels or switches for those.
- ☑ Location of septic tank (if any) and master water valve for house. Find out where pets are buried, so children don't encounter surprises.
- ☑ Obtain special instructions for landscape plants.
- ☑ Identification of doors that are keyed differently from the other doors. Make sure you get copies of all keys at closing. Change all locks after closing. This is usually cheaper if you have the old keys.

☑ Find out the requirements at your children's new school and make sure everyone is familiar with the new neighborhood

Your children will be a big focus of your attention at this point. Now's the time to find out all the requirements for their new schools. Any documents you'll need, such as immunization records, should be copied and put in your moving box. Don't forget—this is an extremely stressful time for your children, also. Take some extra time to drive them around and visit local attractions they might enjoy after the move, such as a playground, ice cream shop, or sports facility. For youngsters, you should take them over to the new house at least two or three times before closing in order to walk around the neighborhood with them. This will help them feel more comfortable, and will keep them from getting lost once you move. If you have pets that can be put on leashes, be sure to include them in these orientation sessions.

Speaking of children and pets, moving day is not a time for them to be included in family activities. Best of all would be a relative who can watch them for a day or two. Barring that, try to find day care for the children and boarding facilities for the animals. Whatever it costs, it will save you money on nerve medicine.

☑ Prepare all change of address notices

Prepare all your change of address notices before you pack. Once you start packing, not very much else will get done. Most magazines can be forwarded by going to one of the online services such as **www.changeofaddressform.com**. Do everything on the same day, so nothing is forgotten.

☑ Send an introduction to your new neighbors

While you're doing paperwork kinds of things, take some time to write a letter to the neighbors, introducing yourself and your family. You know they'll be curious, and it will help break the ice in order to let them know you're friendly. Include all your names, the ages of the children, breeds of the pets, and a little bit of information to help them strike up a conversation, such as hobbies or other interests. Make copies, but if you have small children, mail the intros to just the two neighbors on either side of you, and the one across the street. Mass mailings just aren't a good idea, for obvious reasons. Before you mail them, be sure to check with the current owner of the home to make sure they've told everybody they're moving.

☑ Begin packing

Okay, this is the part you've been putting off—packing. The good news is, there are some things that absolutely, positively, must not be packed. The following items should be dumped into your moving box, for easy access afterwards. They include—cell phone chargers, computer cables, and at least one regular telephone. Also include prescription medicine; over-the-counter medicine you take regularly, like decongestants, aspirin, or heartburn tablets; and, routine grooming items like shampoo, deodorant, shaving cream, etc. One telephone book, one calendar, and any address book you have will go into the box, as will children's schedules and anything important enough to be taped to the refrigerator. Toss in a hammer, screwdrivers (common and Phillips), tape measure, and a pair of pliers, because it's guaranteed you'll need them for something.

If you can think of other things that you'll need on a moment's notice, with no time to find which box they're in, then keep them out as well. Things like jewelry, photo albums, china, and computers may also be good items to travel in the car with you.

☑ Buy colored tags and labels

After pulling out all the no-pack things, it's time to get down to business. Life will be much easier if you invest in some colored address labels, colored tags on string, a large black marker, and a clipboard. You'll want one color for each room in your new home—red means kitchen, green means master bedroom, and so on.

Number each box, marking the number on all four sides and the top. That's because if you label one side, that will usually be the side facing away from you when you're hunting for something later. Put some paper on the clipboard and enter the number for each box, and the contents of that box. You don't want to label boxes themselves because you don't want strangers knowing everything you own; you don't have time to label contents on four sides and the top, so it won't get done; and if, heaven forbid, something is stolen, lost, or destroyed, the label on the box won't help you at all. Writing a list of contents on boxes can be problematic for three reasons.

1. You don't want strangers knowing everything you own.
2. You don't have time to write everything on all four sides and the top.
3. If, heaven forbid, something is stolen, lost, or destroyed, the label on the (missing) box won't help you at all.

Use a clipboard to keep track of the inventory sheets, because a notebook is harder to handle unless you can find one with a firm back cover.

Next, slap a colored address label on all four sides and top of each box, corresponding with the room where the box should be delivered. Some moving employees can't read, and even those who can will thank you for making things so simple. Otherwise, all boxes will be deposited wherever it's easiest, or you'll spend the entire day as a frazzled traffic director. Even if you're moving yourself, with no helpers, you'll find that this system will save you lots of time because you won't have to stop, read the contents of each box, and then make a decision about where to place it. Use the same system for furniture, attaching colored tags to several highly visible places on each piece. Now, all you have to do is write up a guide to give the supervisor or to tape on the door everybody will be using, and you're good to go.

☑ Moving day

☑ Put all your important items in your moving box
☑ Pack an ice chest
☑ Move!

It's here! Hopefully, you are as well prepared as any NFL football coach ready for Super Bowl kickoff. At this point, it should be smooth sailing—hard work, of course, but relatively stress-free.

All the way up to moving day, monitor the weather reports. If rain is anticipated, start making plans to either reschedule or to minimize water problems. You'll need plastic runners to cover high-traffic areas on carpets. Home improvement stores typically sell them in huge rolls, so buy as many feet as you need. Wax the surfaces of wood furniture really well. Don't pack any sheets, bedspreads, or quilts, so you can use them to cover upholstered furniture as the pieces are being carried into the home. Put several rolls of paper towels in your move box, for emergency cleanup.

☑ Put all your important items in your moving box

Put your clipboard, with box contents and color-coding scheme, in your moving box. Make sure your moving box goes in a safe place and won't be accidentally taken by movers or overzealous friends. Check out hiding places like the dishwasher to make sure nothing's been forgotten.

☑ Pack an ice chest

Pack the ice chest with drinks and sandwiches. Yes, everybody will probably take a break for lunch or dinner, but you don't need to count on getting away at the same time. You'll be ready for a little peace and quiet at that point, and may need to reevaluate how the move's going and think of additional instructions for everyone when they return.

☑ Move!

If you're lucky enough to not be part of the manual labor team, your job will be to supervise everything, watch for damage that may be insured so you can make good notes, and issue last-minute instructions for all the little surprises that are inevitable.

Share Your Experience

Was this book helpful? Did I leave anything out? Do you have experiences you want to share with me or questions you want to ask? Do you wish you could find a book on a particular real estate subject, if only someone would write it? Drop me a line at checklists@deniselevans.com.

I promise, I'll answer. Thank you for buying this book, and be sure to look for my other titles for your other real estate needs.

Denise Evans

Appendix A:
Resources

There's simply so much involved in buying a new home that it is virtually impossible to do more than just hit the high points. For more depth on particular subjects, the following resources can prove invaluable.

FINANCIAL TOOLS AND CALCULATORS:

www.cheapskatemonthly.com

http://office.microsoft.com/en-us/templates/default.aspx

www.bankrate.com

Sharp, Hewlett-Packard, and Casio all have good financial calculators for under $35.

CREDIT REPORTS AND CREDIT SCORES:

Annual Credit Report Request Service

P.O. Box 105283

Atlanta, GA 30348

877-322-8228

www.annualcreditreport.com

Even if you are ineligible for a free report, this is the safest avenue to order one directly from the credit reporting agencies. Otherwise, you might end up in the wrong person's database.

DO NOT USE www.freecreditreport.com.

FAIR CREDIT REPORTING ACT AND INFORMATION ABOUT CREDIT REPORTS AND SCORES:

Go to **www.gpoaccess.gov/uscode**, and then enter "15usc1681c" in the search box under 2000 Edition, Supplement 2.

Federal Trade Commission

Consumer Response Center

600 Pennsylvania NW

H-130

Washington, DC 20580

877-382-4357

www.ftc.gov/credit

HOUSING AND LENDING, GENERALLY:

U.S. Department of Housing and Urban Development
202-708-1112
www.hud.gov

INSURANCE:

Find the Insurance Commissioner for your state by going to **www.naic.org/state_web_map.htm**.

Call National Association of Insurance Commisioners at 816-842-3600 for directory assistance.

Insurance score on self: go to **www.choicetrust.com** and click on "Home Insurance Score," or call 866-312-8076.

Insurance claims history on any property: go to **www.choicetrust.com**, and then click on "C.L.U.E.® Reports."

Flood insurance maps: **www.msc.fema.gov**.

Insurance ratings: **www.ambest.com**, or call 908-439-2200, ext. 5742.

Informal insurance ratings: **www.badfaithinsurance.org**.

Private Mortgage Insurance: **www.ftc.gov/bcp/conline/pubs/alerts/pmialrt.htms** or call 877-382-4367.

"FOR SALE BY OWNER" WEBSITES:

www.forsalebyowner.com

www.homesbyowner.com

www.homesalez.com

www.fsbo.com

HOME INSPECTIONS:

National Association of Home Inspectors: **www.nahi.org**

National Association of Certified Home Inspectors: **www.nachi.org**

MANUFACTURED HOUSING:

www.hud.gov/offices/hsg/sfh/mhs/mhshome.cfm

800-927-2891

HOUSEBOATS:

www.houseboatmagazine.com

800-638-0135

LEGAL FORMS:

www.uslegalforms.com

877-389-0141

CONSTRUCTION ESTIMATING SOFTWARE AND BOOKS:

www.craftsman-book.com

800-829-8123

TAXES AND HOME OWNERSHIP:

www.irs.gov/publications

800-TAX-FORM (ask for IRS Publication 530: Tax Information)

For first-time home buyers: **www.irs.gov/individuals/ article/0,,id=96196,00.html** (tax calculator).

You can obtain mailed, or downloadable publications on the following topics.

Publication 530: Tax Information for First Time Homebuyers

Publication 936: Home Mortgage Interest Deduction

Publication 523: Selling Your Home (useful for insights into seller motivation)

Publication 587: Business Use of Your Home

Publication 527: Residential Rental Property (in case you buy a duplex or four-plex to live in one part and rent out the rest)

Topic 504: Home Mortgage Points

Appendix B:
Crash Course on Financing

- ☑ Overview of mortgage lending
- ☑ Explanation of points
- ☑ Loan size underwriting
- ☑ Common lender traps
- ☑ Prepayment penalties
- ☑ Full amortizing loans
- ☑ Balloon loans
- ☑ Variable rate, or ARM, loans
- ☑ Interest-only loans
- ☑ Growing equity mortgages
- ☑ No-document loans
- ☑ What is the right loan arrangement for you?
- ☑ VA guaranteed loans
- ☑ FHA insured loans
- ☑ USDA loans
- ☑ HUD Section 184 loan guarantees for Native Americans
- ☑ Fannie Mae, Ginnie Mae, and Freddie Mac
- ☑ Mortgages from stock brockerage houses
- ☑ Assumable loans
- ☑ Creative financing sources
- ☑ Beware of these lending alternatives

If you're not entirely comfortable with lending concepts and practices, you won't be comfortable shopping for the best mortgage rates and terms. You'll want to get the process over with as quickly as possible. This is normal, but it can be very expensive in the short term and the long run. Following is a plain-English, no-nonsense guide that will unlock the mysteries of mortgage financing and help you make the best possible decisions.

You can ask intelligent questions and make informed choices if you have a little bit of background information about the mortgage loan industry. The following information will hit the high points for you. Entire books are devoted to this subject if you desire additional assistance.

☑ Overview of mortgage lending

Most mortgage loans come from one of the following sources: banks, mortgage companies, brokers, savings banks, or credit unions (all called *conventional loans*), or with assistance from government programs such as the Federal Housing Administration (FHA), U.S. Department of Veterans Affairs (VA), or Rural Housing Services (RHS). The terms *conventional* and *government* are applied depending on whether there's any government involvement insuring or guaranteeing the loan, even if a conventional bank actually loans the funds. In rare circumstances, the government will actually make loans directly to homebuyers.

The common expressions *conforming* and *nonconforming* are used to describe whether or not the loans follow guidelines set down by Fannie Mae and Freddie Mac (more below on these two corporations).

To further complicate the vocabulary, almost all loans are *originated* in one place—called the primary market—and then sold to others in what's called the *secondary market*. The two largest purchasers of home loans are Fannie Mae and

Freddie Mac. Although they don't directly loan any money to borrowers, their strength as buyers allows them to effectively set the underwriting requirements for mortgage loans. That is because they will not buy any loans that don't meet their guidelines. Loans must conform to their requirements, or Fannie Mae and Freddie Mac won't buy them. Lenders need to sell their loans, so they'll have more cash to loan out on more mortgages.

The largest single-family loan Fannie Mae will buy is $417,000, with some exceptions for particular geographic areas. For Freddie Mac, it's $359,650. Anything larger can't be bundled into the standard resale packages. This is important to you because you can generally receive cheaper interest rates if you qualify for a Fannie Mae or Freddie Mac resale of your loan. If you're slightly over the top loan limits, you might want to pay a somewhat larger down payment in order to come within the requirements. Larger loans, often called *jumbo loans* or *nonconforming loans*, are usually kept in the lender's private portfolio, or charged higher interest rates and sold to other types of investors. There's nothing derogatory about a nonconforming loan.

☑ Explanation of points

Borrowers typically pay *points* in connection with a mortgage loan. One point is equal to one percent of the loan. A fee of one point on a $150,000 loan would be $1,500. The money can be used for a wide variety of things, so it's important to find out the purpose of the points, as well as the amount, when comparing loans. There are two varieties—*origination points* and *discount points*. Origination points cover closing expenses and fees, including the mortgage broker's profit. Many of the fees covered by origination points are really just disguised additional profit for the broker and the lender, and are completely negotiable. Discount points are used to *buy down* your interest rate, because you are prepaying some of the interest with the discount points. How much you can reduce your interest rate varies with the type of loan and market conditions at the time. Typically, though, you will have to make mortgage payments for several years before you start saving money because of the buy-down. You'll need to evaluate how long you'll own your home to see if discount points make sense for you.

Here's an example of how that works. Suppose you want to borrow $100,000 on a thirty-year fixed-rate mortgage. You think you can get a 7% interest rate with no discount points, or you can save ¼ of a percent if you pay one point. The one discount point will cost you $1,000.

Monthly payment @ 7.00%	$665.30
Monthly payment @ 6¾%	$648.60
Monthly savings	$16.70

At a savings of $16.70 per month, it will take you 59.88 months, or almost exactly five years, to save enough money to reimburse yourself for the $1,000 paid in points. Will you be in the home that long? Probably not. This is just one of the many ways lenders make money from unwary borrowers.

☑ Loan size underwriting

Most people think, "If I prequalify for a loan, that's how much I can afford to spend." This is false, false, false! Lenders are in the business of renting money to you. They will stretch an incredibly huge amount in order to justify loaning you as much money as possible. Underwriting calculations regarding what you can afford each month might assume you never eat out, never buy clothing, will not want any new furniture, that you are always healthy, will never need any repairs, and take public transportation to work. Just because your lender's willing for you to have an impoverished lifestyle in luxury surroundings doesn't mean you should go along with the idea.

The most important factors that lenders look at when making loan decisions are credit score, employment history, and net worth—in that order—and *then* they evaluate how much of your income must be devoted to cover housing costs. Those financing guidelines will determine whether you get the loan, for how much, and at what interest rate and origination fees.

To determine maximum purchase price they think you can afford, lenders compare *PITI* (principal, interest, taxes, and insurance for a proposed home loan) to your monthly income. The traditional rule was that PITI could not exceed 28% of your monthly take-home pay. In other words, if your take home was $5,000 a month, PITI could not exceed $1,400 a month. If debt service, taxes, and insurance exceeded this number, you would not qualify for a loan.

Some lenders use a different formula and include utilities and other loan obligations in their calculations. The ratio they rely on says that PITI plus utilities and installment debt cannot exceed 36% of monthly take-home pay. *Installment debt* is defined as anything that has more than ten or twelve months (depending on the lender) left to pay— such as a car note or student loan. If you have a car payment, but the car will be paid off in ten months, they don't count it. One of the shortcomings of this approach is related to the installment debt issue. Just because your car is going to be paid off in ten months doesn't mean you're not going to buy a new car at the end. You might still have installment debt, but it will not be included by the banker when he or she calculates how much mortgage you could afford.

☑ Common lender traps

Theoretically, mortgage brokers shop the market in order to find the best deal for you. Sometimes, it doesn't actually work that way, and the broker is looking out for his or her best interests—not yours. Loan officers can also be guilty of sharp practices, downright fraud, or simple laziness, even though it might not directly benefit them. Beware of each group, keep your eyes open, and question everything. Here are a few examples of bad practices.

- *Bait and switch rates.* The broker or lender quotes one rate, but once you're too deeply committed to back out, tells you something has happened so you are not eligible for the cheap interest. As a general rule of thumb, if someone quotes a rate that's ½% lower than anyone else's deal with comparable terms, then it's probably too good to be true. Ask for written quotes, and the underwriting requirements to qualify for that rate. In addition, obtain a written estimate of all fees and third-party expenses you will have to pay in connection with the loan. Discounted interest rates could be more than offset by extremely high up-front fees.

- *No-fee loans with hidden fees.* Sometimes lenders will pay the origination points on a loan, so the borrower does not have to pay them. These are then advertised as "no fee" loans, but they're really "zero points" loans. The fees for various things such as credit review, underwriting analysis, flood zone verification, and so on, can be substantial. By federal law, some or all of such fees must be treated as additional interest for purposes of calculating the *Truth In Lending* figure called the annual percentage rate, or APR. This is different from the *face rate* on the note, which is the rate usually quoted to you in sales pitches. When shopping, ask for a written estimate of the APR for the size and term loan you are requesting. If the APR is substantially higher than the quoted interest rate, then there are some fees you should know about before making any decisions.

- *The disappearing rate lock.* Most brokers and lenders will commit to a certain interest rate for a short period of time. If the loan doesn't close within that time, your rate could go up. You can agree to pay additional fees or points and *lock* your interest rate for a longer period. Even if interest rates rise in the meantime, you still get the benefit of your locked rate, assuming you close on time. Some dishonest brokers charge you the lock fee, but then keep the money rather than paying the actual lender in order to lock the rate. They're gambling that rates won't increase in the meantime. If you obtain a lock, ask for written confirmation from the actual lender, not from the mortgage broker.

- *Interest rates that don't drop with the market.* If you're quoted one rate and then, before you lock, the market increases, you'll have to pay the higher interest rate. On the other hand, if interest rates fall in the time between your application and your lock, some lenders and brokers won't tell you. They'll just "let" you pay the higher-than-market interest rate, unless you challenge it. Don't quit tracking interest rates once you put in an application.

- *Interest rates that increase to an artificial market.* You might receive a quote for a low interest rate that will increase to "market" after a period of time. The problem is, loan documents might define "market" as something artificial and completely within the control of the lender, no matter what the rest of the United States is doing. Lenders can make the market—and your interest rate—whatever they want. The thing that defines the market is called the *index.* At the time of your loan application, the lender should disclose to you what it they will be using. Commonly acceptable ones are Constant Maturity Treasury (CMT), Treasury Bill (T-Bill), 12-Month Treasury Average (MTA), and London Inter Bank Offering Rate (LIBOR). If your index is not on this list, investigate further. There are many other reputable ones.

- *Fake expenses.* You might be charged fees that are really just additional profit to the broker or lender. You may encounter a great variety of fees for things such as underwriting, document preparation, credit review, and appraisal review. These are completely negotiable and can be waived if you insist. The federal government does not have hard and fast rules about what fees must be treated as interest for purposes of calculating the APR, and lenders have some leeway regarding what to include. Just because you ask for an estimated APR and it turns out to be very close to the quoted interest rate, doesn't mean there won't be a lot of lender fees at closing. Always ask for a list of expenses, a good faith estimate of the amount, and a statement regarding whether they are paid to the lender, the broker, or an independent third party.

- *Borrowers with less than perfect credit paying very high interest rates.* You usually know if your credit isn't perfect. You are psychologically prepared to be turned down for financing, or to pay a higher interest rate than other people. Brokers sometimes take advantage of this by quoting you a higher rate than the one you actually qualify for. The broker receives a fee based on the difference between the interest you should be paying and the rate you agreed to. This is called the *yield spread premium*. Used properly, the yield spread premium compensates the broker for services he or she provides to you, and can also be used by the broker to fund certain closing costs that might be too expensive for you. In other words, you might agree to pay a higher interest rate in order to not have any closing costs. Used improperly, the practice amounts to price gouging and is predatory. Almost every state has class action litigation going on over undisclosed yield spread premiums. To protect yourself, ask how the broker will be paid, and in what amount. Remember, loan brokers do need to make a living or they'd be out on the beach instead of sitting in the office with you. Not all fees are suspect.

☑ Prepayment penalties

Some loans contain provisions requiring you to pay a penalty if you pay the loan off earlier than agreed, or if you make larger principal reductions than the lender planned. If there is a penalty, it's generally only during the first few years of the loan. Sometimes it's a percentage of the loan balance at that time, other times it's six to twelve months' interest. The reasoning is that lenders count on receiving an income stream for a certain period of time. If they receive their principal early, then they must loan it to someone else as quickly as possible. That might not happen immediately, and it will almost certainly require some marketing and administrative expenses. Fortunately, most consumer loans do not have a prepayment penalty.

☑ Fully amortizing loans

The most common type of mortgage loan today is called *fully amortizing*, meaning the regular monthly payments will eventually pay the loan, in full, over a specified amount of time. Thirty-year terms are the most widespread, although some longer terms are now allowed, such as forty- and fifty-year mortgages. Many people urge shorter loan terms in order to save interest. Over the course of thirty years, a $100,000 mortgage at 6% interest will result in $115,838 in interest, with payments of $599.55 per month. For the recommended twenty-year term, total interest drops to $71,943 but payments increase to $716.43 per month.

Most Americans keep their homes less than ten years. So, as a practical matter, the property is sold and the loan paid off long before the completion of the term.

☑ Balloon loans

Balloon mortgages allow a fixed interest rate, giving you stability in your financial affairs, but the entire loan will be due in five or seven years. Because the lender's potential exposure to below-market rates on your loan is limited in time, it can offer you somewhat lower rates than might otherwise be possible on a thirty-year mortgage. Many times, you have the option to *convert* the loan to a regular mortgage at the market rate for thirty-year loans, *plus* a little bit of extra interest, usually 0.375%. If you have a five-year balloon with a conversion option, the loan is called a *5/25 Convertible*. For seven-year balloons, it's called a *7/23 Convertible*.

☑ Variable rate, or ARM, loans

Variable rate loans initially have a lower interest rate than fixed rate mortgages, by about one half to one percentage point. The difference on a $100,000, thirty-year mortgage, at 5% instead of 6%, is about $60 per month. For some buyers, this amount can make the difference in whether they can afford a home or not, or what size they can qualify for.

The downside of an ARM is that the rate changes every so often—usually one, three, or five years, although it can be more frequent. The time interval it must remain unchanged is called the *adjustment period*. At the end of an adjustment period, the rate can increase or decrease, depending on what's happening with interest rates nationwide.

Any time you obtain an ARM loan, you should know the maximum amount the rate can increase in any year (*periodic cap*), and the most it can increase, in total during the term of the loan (*overall cap*). Most commonly, an ARM has a limit of 1% per year increases, and the rate can never be more than 5% higher than the initial one. Although this cap is common, it's not required. Be sure to ask lots of questions about caps. By law, almost all adjustable rate mortgages must have an overall cap in some amount.

Some ARM loans have *payment caps*, meaning your monthly payment cannot increase above a certain amount, even if the interest rate rises sharply. This is common with mortgages that do not have periodic caps, only overall caps. The danger is something called *negative amortization*. Suppose your payment cap is $500 per month, but your interest rate increase should have resulted in a payment of $550 per month. Your lender doesn't just forgive the extra $50 in interest. No, your lender takes that $50 per month out of your equity! Rather than amortizing your loan, so the principal balance gets lower each month, you are negatively amortizing and your principal balance is getting higher every month!

It is common for ARM loans to offer really low initial rates, called *discounted rates*, combined with large *points*, or initial loan fees. Very large discounts are usually arranged by the seller of a property, who pays your lender a fee in order to obtain a lower interest rate for you. Payment sticker shock could set in when the rate increases to market, which could be 2% to 3% in additional interest.

Convertible ARMs can be converted to fixed-rate mortgages at your option. There's usually a fee for the conversion, so you should find out the amount before you agree to the loan.

☑ Interest-only loans

Many lenders have been aggressively marketing interest-only loans. The upside for the borrower is that monthly interest payments are as low as possible. Lenders like this, because more people qualify for loans based on mortgage-payment-to-income ratios required by underwriters. The downside is that the loan balance doesn't decrease, and there's usually a balloon or a conversion to full amortization in five to ten years. In order to be successful, the arrangement absolutely depends on real estate prices increasing steadily every year, so you can sell or refinance when the balloon comes due. In the alternative, with the conversion type of interest-only loan, you must be financially capable, in the future, of making payments on what will essentially be a twenty-year loan instead of a thirty-year loan. To clarify, if you have a thirty-year interest only mortgage with a ten-year conversion, you will not make any principal reductions for the first ten years. Beginning in year eleven, you will have to begin paying down the loan, so that it's paid off in the remaining twenty years of the term. This will result in substantially higher payments than previously. For a $250,000 mortgage at 6% interest, the monthly payments for the first ten years will be only $1,250. For the next twenty years, they will be $1,791.08 per month.

Most financial planners caution against interest-only mortgage loans. You have huge risks of foreclosure if the market takes a downturn in general, your neighborhood declines in value, or your earnings do not increase substantially over the years so you can afford the much higher payments. Traditionally, the arrangement made sense for people with a small monthly income but large periodic bonuses or commissions they could use to pay down principal. It was also popular for affluent borrowers when the stock market was at its height. Wealthy borrowers would take the money they saved on monthly payments, invest it in stocks, and earn 15% to 20% on their funds. At the end of each year they would sell some stock, pay down the mortgage balance and pocket the profit. This isn't recommended—it's just how it used to work.

For most Americans, the savings on an interest-only mortgage are simply not worth the risk. Monthly payments on a $250,000 interest-only loan at 6% interest are $1,250. The same loan, fully amortizing over thirty years, results in monthly payments of $1,498. After three years of an interest-only loan, you will have built up no additional equity in your home. With the fully amortizing loan, you will have paid off almost $10,000 of your loan after three years.

☑ Growing equity mortgages

A growing equity mortgage (GEM) is a fixed-rate mortgage, but with scheduled increases in monthly payments over time. As the payments increase, the excess money is applied to reduce the principal balance of a loan. It gives borrowers the benefits of the low initial payments possible with thirty-year mortgages, but the lower overall interest costs and faster equity buildup found in twenty- or twenty-five-year mortgages, all without having to refinance periodically. The GEMs on condos and town homes are eligible for FHA insurance, providing borrowers with good interest rates and low up-front costs. There are some limitations for apartment-to-condo conversions. The conversion must have occurred at least one year earlier. In addition, the borrower must have been a tenant at the time of the conversion, or a majority of the tenants must have voted for the conversion. Finally, at least 80% of the FHA-insured loans in the project must be to owner-occupants.

☑ No-document loans

The so-called *no-doc mortgages* are usually more accurately called *low-document mortgages*. They're usually recommended for people who don't have traditional W-2 tax forms for income verification.

Warning!
Some mortgage brokers will push you into a no-doc loan program with higher down payment requirements and higher interest rates, even though you might qualify for a traditional loan with a little extra work. Tax returns for the last two years, bank statements, or letters from employers might be enough documentation to get the cheaper interest rates.

A wide variety of people might not have the ability, or the desire, to share their financial information with a lender. At one end of the spectrum are people who work for cash and don't report very much of it to the IRS—we don't recommend the practice, but it does happen with a great deal of frequency. The other extreme consists of people with complicated financial lives that support very nice lifestyles, but a wide variety of tax write-offs that result in income tax losses every year. It's a little difficult to fit into the requirements for a conforming loan on a $300,000 condo when you have no W-2s and your tax returns for the last three years seem to indicate you're losing about $250,000 per year. Still other people have substantial assets they simply don't want to disclose to anyone, for privacy reasons.

There are three main types of low-doc/no-doc mortgages. The *stated income mortgage* is usually for self-employed people or ones who make their living from commissions or tips. A *no-ratio loan* means the borrower can't fit within the loan-to-income ratios because they have complicated financial lives or they're in a transition time and between jobs or marriages. This might be appropriate for someone with very little income, but who receives huge child support payments each month, or for someone who lives off their investments. Finally, the true no-doc or *NINA* (no income/no asset verification) is for the most creditworthy people who aren't willing to share any financial information at all, but are willing to pay the price tag through higher interest rates.

☑ What is the right loan arrangement for you?

Traditional fixed-rate mortgages tend to be the safest loans for buyers since the interest rate is locked for the entire term of the mortgage. When mortgage rates are at or near historic lows, it's a good idea to take out a fixed-rate loan.

Adjustable-rate mortgages (ARMs) have lower initial interest rates than fixed rate alternatives, but the borrower bears the risk of rising interest rates in the future. ARMs are most appropriate when mortgage rates are high, but expected to decline in the future. The lower initial rates on ARMs make it easier to qualify for a loan since lenders base their loan decision on the size of your initial loan payment.

When shopping for adjustable rate loans, look for loans that have the longest adjustment interval if you think interest rates will increase in the coming years. Loans with interest rates that adjust every three years are usually better than loans that can be adjusted annually. With some ARMs, you can lock in the rate for up to ten years. All adjustable loans have interest rate caps that limit the size of the interest rate adjustment. The smaller the interest rate cap, the better. The same goes for the initial interest. The lower the beginning interest rate on the ARM, relative to the rates on fixed rate loans, the better.

ARMs can be particularly attractive for buyers who don't expect to be living in their home for more than ten years or so. If you play your cards right, by the time the interest rate on your ARM catches up to what you would have paid on a fixed-rate loan, you will have probably sold your home. Even if you decide to stay long-term, it should be possible to refinance when interest rates moderate.

Used wisely, interest-only loans can get you into your home sooner and with less strain on your budget, at least in the early years of the loan. If you are planning to live in your property for the rest of you life, make sure you will be able to handle the higher payments once debt reduction begins. Retirees, who do not anticipate significant income increases in the years to come, should probably avoid interest-only loans.

☑ VA guaranteed loans

The Veterans Administration will *guarantee* certain loans made by banks or other lenders to qualified veterans, up to a maximum amount of $50,750; they don't actually loan the money directly. Most lenders require that the VA guarantee, plus any down payment, equal at least 25% of the value (or purchase price, whichever is less) of the home. The eligibility rules for length of service are rather complicated, and range from ninety days to six years, depending on the circumstances, timing, war time or peace time, and the veteran's status as active duty, National Guard, etc. For more information, contact the Veterans Administration at **www.va.gov** or 800-827-1000.

With a VA guarantee, lenders can approve somewhat riskier loans, at lower interest rates, and with little or no down payment. In addition, borrowers can qualify even though up to 41% of their income is used for debt service. This is higher than typical underwriting requirements for non-VA loans.

The borrower must live in the home and not use it for rental income, be a satisfactory credit risk (under lenient VA guidelines), and have a stable source of income. In order to obtain the guarantee, the veteran will usually have to pay a 2% fee, and eligible Reserve/National Guard members will have to pay a 2.75% fee. These fees can be reduced by paying a down payment; any lender or broker can help you with the details.

You will need a Certificate of Eligibility. If you don't already have one, it can be obtained from your local VA office by completing VA Form 26-1880; "Request for Determination of Eligibility and Available Loan Guaranty Entitlement." You'll also need a VA appraisal, called a *Certificate of Reasonable Value* (CRV). The lender usually orders that. Otherwise, the process is pretty much the same as it is for any other loan, except that you must advise your lender that you want a VA guarantee. They don't read minds, you know!

☑ FHA insured loans

The *Federal Housing Administration* (FHA) is a part of the *Department of Housing and Urban Development* (HUD). The FHA has a goal of increasing home ownership among low-income and middle-income Americans. To encourage that, it insures certain loans made by conventional lenders. The FHA does not make any loans, itself. Because of the insurance, though, lenders are able to stretch a bit and loan money to people who might not otherwise qualify.

These loans are not limited to borrowers with credit problems or low income, but they do assist those who might otherwise not be able to obtain financing. If there are financial blemishes in your life, these are the requirements: Qualified borrowers must have been discharged from bankruptcy at least two years earlier, been paying on a Chapter 13 plan for at least twelve months, or had a foreclosure no more recently than three years earlier. All judgments must have been paid in full before closing, but collections accounts don't have to be paid if you have *mitigating factors* (a legally good excuse). Usually, you must have a history of four or more creditors with regular payments on your credit report. If you don't have that many, you can use evidence of timely rent payments, utilities, or car insurance.

The required down payment is usually only 3%, and the money can be a gift from someone else. There's an exception for homeowners who lost their property in presidentially-designated federal disaster areas—they can obtain 100% financing. Disaster victims do not have to buy property in their same area; they can relocate, if they want.

If you still don't qualify because of credit problems, you can add a co-borrower with good credit to the loan—they don't have to actually occupy the property with you. There is a limit on closing costs that can be charged to the borrower. The size of an FHA insured loan is limited, though, ranging from a current high of $172,632 in some parts of the country, to a high of $362,790 in others. To check your limits, visit **https://entp.hud.gov/idapp/html/hicostlook.cfm**.

Other than eligibility, the basic difference between a VA *guaranteed* loan and an FHA *insured* loan is the thing that comes with all insurance—an insurance premium. The VA does not impose an insurance premium, because it's a guarantee program. On the other hand, it does charge a funding fee, so it's not like you get off scot-free. The Department of Housing and Urban Development does charge a mortgage insurance premium, but you can finance it by combining it into the total loan. The normal FHA mortgage insurance premium is 1.5% of the purchase price, which is paid up front but can be rolled into the loan. There's also a monthly mortgage insurance premium of 0.5%. The monthly insurance payment drops off completely when you reach certain equity levels, usually

78%. An FHA loan is assumable, if the new borrower otherwise meets all requirements.

The FHA has some other, specialized loan programs for particular classes of borrowers. The *Teacher Next Door* program offers up to a 50% discount off the asking price for homes being sold by HUD, if you're a teacher living in the neighborhood in which you teach. There's a similar incentive for law enforcement officers who live in the community where they work—*Officer Next Door*. When an FHA-insured borrower defaults and the lender has to foreclose, HUD buys the home from the lender, and then tries to resell it as quickly as possible.

For more information, visit **www.hud.gov**, or call the Department of Housing and Urban Development customer service center at 800-767-7468.

☑ USDA loans

The United States Department of Agriculture offers direct loans, and loan guarantees, for people living in rural areas. We frequently think of such loans as being for farms only, but that's not true.

The Section 502 Rural Development Direct Loans offer mortgage money that comes directly from the USDA. They are generally available to low- and very-low-income borrowers, who can obtain 100% financing for up to thirty-eight years. Mortgage payments are based on income. More information is available at **www.rurdev.usda.gov**.

USDA-guaranteed loans are available for low and moderate income borrowers, providing 100% financing in qualified rural areas. First time homebuyers must take a homebuyers education course if their credit score is below 660. To find out if you, or your property, is eligible, visit **http://eligibility.sc. egov.usda.gov**, or call 800-414-1226 and ask for the service center for your part of the country.

☑ HUD Section 184 loan guarantees for Native Americans

The HUD Section 184 Loan Guarantees for Native Americans program was enacted in 1992. It is designed to make home ownership possible on Indian reservation lands, and in Indian or Native Alaskan areas that are off-reservation. It is limited to Native Americans. The problem with Indian reservations is that the U.S. government owns all the land, in trust, for the Native Americans. This makes it a little difficult to borrow money from a bank. While a great many of you reading this book won't be eligible, those who are probably have a difficult time finding financing. In addition, this should give hope to all the rest of you that, if you look hard enough, no matter what your circumstances, you'll find a loan program that fits you.

Under the HUD 184 program, money is made available from traditional lenders, who offer federally guaranteed loans. Loans are administered by the Department of Housing and Urban Development. For more information, call 800-561-5913, or visit **www.hud.gov/offices/pih/ih/homeownership/184**.

☑ Fannie Mae, Ginnie Mae, and Freddie Mac

Most mortgage loans are combined into huge packages and then sold to large investors—like pension funds and insurance companies—or they are *securitized* and people can invest in the pools, much like a mutual fund. In order to encourage investment, and thus make more money available for additional mortgage loans, the U.S. government established a variety of programs.

The federal government established the Federal National Mortgage Association—commonly called Fannie Mae—in 1938. It made no loans, but was authorized to buy FHA-insured loans from lenders. In 1968, President Lyndon Johnson ordered it converted to a private company with private investors, because the Vietnam Conflict was such a burden on the national budget that it could no longer afford Fannie Mae. Today, it still makes no direct loans for home mortgages, but simply buys mortgages on the open market, pools them, and then sells them as *mortgage-backed securities*. Fannie Mae is traded on the New York Stock Exchange.

At the same time that Fannie Mae was privatized, Congress carved out part of its functions, placed them under the control of the Department of Housing and Urban Development, and named the new entity the Government National Mortgage Association. Ginnie Mae, as it's called, guarantees pools of federally-insured or federally-guaranteed loans. Even if a borrower defaults, the investors will still receive their monthly principal and interest payments, in full. Contrary to popular belief, Ginnie Mae does not buy or sell mortgages and does not issue mortgage-backed securities. There is much disinformation on the Internet on this issue, so be careful.

Congress chartered the Federal Home Loan Mortgage Corporation (FHLMC)—Freddie Mac for short—in 1970, so that Fannie Mae would not have a monopoly on the mortgage loan secondary market. Its purpose was to buy mortgages from lenders, so the lenders would have additional cash to make more loans. After buying the loans, Freddie Mac issues mortgage-related securities that can be bought on the open market. Freddie Mac is listed on the New York Stock Exchange.

☑ Mortgages from stock brokerage houses

Recently, stock brokerage houses have started loaning money for home mortgages. Usually, there's a high minimum loan amount of at least $100,000. Sometimes, you must have a brokerage account with them. Major players include Charles Schwab and Merrill Lynch, to name two. If you have a stock broker, check with him or her for mortgage loan availability.

☑ Assumable loans

The popular perception of an assumable loan is one that can be taken over by a buyer with no credit check, a minor amount of paperwork, and perhaps a $100 assumption fee. That was true many years ago, until the 20% or more interest rates of the late 1970s and early 1980s, and the savings and loan crisis, forced everybody involved to think twice about the practice. Today, you may be able to find a seller who has a no-questions-asked assumable loan, but it's extremely rare—FHA-insured loans and VA-guaranteed loans are "assumable," but the buyer still has to meet underwriting requirements.

The thing that keeps a loan from being assumable is something called a *due on sale clause*. Almost all mortgage loans contain them. If property is sold, the entire loan balance is due immediately, even if all the payments have been made perfectly on time. Many Internet and other gurus have schemes for getting around due on sale clauses, but don't believe them. So-called *wrap around mortgages* or *all inclusive trust deeds* rely on someone not spilling the beans to the lender.

My philosophy is, if you can't tell someone, don't do it. All such schemes are just that—schemes. A lot smarter minds than you and me have spent the last twenty-five years closing loopholes that allowed assumption without credit checks or any other sort of lender decision making. For the most part, the only time you're possibly going to find a truly old-fashioned assumable loan is if your seller had private financing from an individual, and that individual had poor legal advice when drafting the loan documents.

☑ Creative financing sources

Sometimes, no matter how hard you try, you just won't be able to qualify for an affordable mortgage loan, or you won't be able to raise the down payment. There are still some alternatives for you.

The first is to ask the seller if he or she will hold a *second mortgage* for a limited amount of time. Be careful, though, because some loan programs prohibit you from obtaining second mortgages. The thinking is, the higher monthly payments from a first and a second mortgage create more of a financial burden, and make it more likely that you will default on one or both loans. Be sure to ask your lenders and brokers about this option.

Private mortgage insurance (PMI) is available for people who cannot afford the typical 20% down payment required for a home purchase. A separate company insures your lender, up to 30% of the amount of your loan, in case you default. If the lender forecloses, the insurer pays off, up to its limits. As a practical matter, the PMI company usually simply pays the lender in full and then takes over the foreclosed property. Insurance premiums are paid by the borrower, and can be pretty stout. Sometimes you pay the premium in full, at closing. Other times you pay the annual fee at closing, and then pay an additional amount every month. Be aware that, in all likelihood, no one will contact in several years to tell you that your loan balance is now low enough so you don't need PMI any more. You'll need to monitor this, and advise someone when the premiums should stop.

The *Homeowners' Protection Act of 1998*, also called the *PMI Act*, requires automatic cancellation of PMI insurance when the loan is paid down to 78% of the original value of the property. Homeowners can request cancellation when the loan is paid down to 80% of the value of the property. There are many exceptions that work for you, and others that work against you. Visit the HUD website at **www.hud.gov/offices/hsg/sfh/res/ respapmi.cfm** for more details.

Seller financing, with the former owner holding a first mortgage on the unit, is sometimes an option. It's typically available in only two situations. One is when the seller has a difficult property and can't get a decent price for it in the conventional manner. He or she will agree to hold the financing, knowing that people with poor credit, having fewer options, will agree to the price just in order to get the easy financing. The other time you'll commonly see seller financing is when someone has no need for cash, but would enjoy earning income higher than he or she could obtain by investing in bank CDs or money market funds. Because of the due on sale clause, seller first-mortgage financing is usually available when the seller has no debt of his or her own on the property. Such sellers are typically retirees moving to smaller homes, or heirs selling their parents' property.

Investment financing is another option. To do this, you find a creditworthy tenant who would like to share the home on a somewhat long-term basis—perhaps under a five-year lease. You obtain from that person a lease commitment for a certain term, at a certain rental rate sufficient to pay the mortgage payments, taxes and insurance, and monthly fees. With that in hand, you can sometimes buy the home as an investment property, based on the creditworthiness of your tenant. You then share the home with your tenant, and pay a portion of the "rent" each month. Interest rates will be somewhat higher than typical home loans, but it is a way to buy a desirable property when all other avenues seem closed to you. You'll have to declare the rental income, but you'll also be able to take depreciation and other expenses. Be aware that this cannot be a sham transaction. If you default, and the lender forecloses, the new purchaser might be entitled to enforce the lease. In addition, you and your tenant will be guilty of bank fraud—a federal crime—if the whole transaction is for appearances' sake only.

☑ Beware of these lending alternatives

Finally, there is one very risky option we do not recommend, but which can be readily found on the Internet and through brokerage channels. This is the financing practice known as *bond for title, bond for deed,* or *land sale contract.* They all work the same way. A third party buys the home you want. You make monthly payments to that third party, usually at extremely high interest rates. You have very limited ability to pay the loan off early if your finances improve to the point you can obtain conventional financing. At the end of the loan term, if you've made all your payments on time, the third party will give you a deed. If you miss one payment, at any point in the process, the third party can declare a default and you lose everything. You have no right to cure the default, no ability to redeem, and limited bankruptcy rights. Most lenders in this arena count on the fact that you will default and they will be able to resell the property to some other person. The practice is so predatory, and has such a statistically high default rate, that many states regulate it heavily. Before pursuing this option, talk to a credit counseling agency in your state, and possibly an attorney.

Appendix C:
Tax Considerations for Home Buyers

The government is firmly committed to promoting home ownership. As a result, it offers a wide variety of tax incentives for homebuyers. Most of them take the form of tax breaks. Some of the more important ones are explained here. For a more thorough treatment of the different subjects, check out the Resources section of this book and call the IRS to request publications or visit their website at **www.irs.gov** to download information.

- ☑ Deducting closing costs
- ☑ *Tax deductions for Home Purchase Expenses*
- ☑ Using IRA or Roth-IRA retirement money for a purchase
- ☑ Using 401(k) money for a home purchase
- ☑ Mortgage interest deduction
- ☑ How much money do you save with interest deductions?
- ☑ Taxes due on a sale of your home

☑ Deducting closing costs

Some closing expenses can be deducted on your tax returns in the same year as your home purchase. Those are in Column A in the chart on page 249. Others have to be added up and divided by the number of years in your loan, and only that small amount can be deducted every year. That's Column B. A few expenses must be added to your *basis*, meaning purchase price, for purposes of determining your profit on a resale. (These may reduce taxable profit on resale.) A purchase of $100,000, with $5,000 worth of things added to basis, means you can sell for $105,000 without showing a profit. Under current tax law, husbands and wives can make a total of $500,000 profit on the sale of their home without paying taxes, but these things are always subject to change. In addition, in rapidly growing markets, you can rack up a $500,000 property value increase pretty quickly, so you'll still be looking for ways to minimize your taxes. As a practical matter, with the $250,000/$500,000 exclusion from income for profit on the sale of a home, you probably will not realize any benefit from these items in Column C.

Tax Deductions for Home Purchase Expenses *			
	A	B	C
Loan origination fee for primary home purchase	•		
Buyer-paid loan discount points for primary home purchase	•		
Seller-paid loan discount points for primary home (but only if the seller doesn't deduct them also)	•		
Any of the above three, but for secondary home		•	
Prepaid interest	•		
Property tax prorates	•		
Title insurance for owner			•
Survey			•
Legal fees for closing			•
Recordation fees and transfer taxes			•
Normal seller expenses you agree to pay, like real estate commission, back taxes, unpaid assessments or dues, etc.			•

For more information, consult IRS Publications 530 (Tax Information for First Time Homeowners); 523 (Selling Your Home); 587 (Business Use of Your Home); and, 936 (Home Mortgage Interest Deduction), available at **www.irs.gov** or by calling 800-829-3676.

　　* See page 248 for explanation of chart.

☑ Using IRA or Roth-IRA retirement money for a purchase

Generally speaking, first-time home buyers can withdraw up to $10,000 from their IRA or Roth-IRA accounts, penalty-free, in order to pay qualified home purchase expenses such as a down payment. Spouses can withdraw up to $20,000. There's a lifetime limit, though. Once you use up your distribution free passes, you can't put the money back in your account and then use it again in the future. Remember, too, you still have to pay taxes on the money, but not the 10% early-withdrawal penalty.

It's important to know the IRS definition of a *first-time home buyer*. It's someone who hasn't bought a home in the last two years, or the spouse, parent, children, or assorted other relatives of such people. In other words, your grandmother can withdraw up to $10,000 from her IRA to help you buy a house as long as you haven't bought one in the last two years!

For more information, go to **www.irs.gov** or call 800-TAX-FORM and get a copy of Tax Topic 428 (Roth IRA Distributions) and Publication 590 (Individual Retirement Accounts).

☑ Using 401(k) money for a home purchase

Although you can't distribute money from your 401(k) program penalty-free or tax-free, you may be able to borrow money from it. This will depend on whether your particular plan documents allow it. In order to qualify for the IRS turning a blind eye, such loans must meet all of the following requirements:

- less then 50% of vested account, or $50,000, whichever is less;
- loan must be repaid within five years (unless to buy your primary residence); and,
- loan payments just be substantially equal, made at least quarterly.

There are some other, technical requirements, such as reductions on the $50,000 limit if you already have outstanding loans from the 401(k). Ask your plan administrator for details.

This is not a recommended source of money unless you have absolutely no other choices. Sure, there's no credit check and the paperwork is easy, but you're taking money out of an investment account that's probably earning a pretty high return. If your problem getting a loan someplace else is bad credit, not bad cash flow, then set up the 401(k) loan so you'll be paying a high interest rate. That way, you compensate for the lost earnings from the money you've taken out.

☑ Mortgage interest deduction

The IRS allows you to deduct home mortgage interest from your income in order to arrive at something called the *adjusted gross income* (AGI). Gross income is usually the same thing as your W-2 income. You actually pay taxes only on the AGI.

There are some limits on the deductibility of home mortgage interest. Currently, only the interest on $1,000,000 worth of mortgage debt is deductible, so if you are planning to buy a $1,500,000 home with 20% down, then your mortgage will be $1,200,000. Only part of your interest will be deductible—the part attributable to $1,000,000. Fortunately, most of us don't need to worry about this problem.

Home equity line of credit interest is deductible on only $100,000 worth of debt. You can have more debt that that, but only the interest on the $100,000 portion can be deducted.

Second home interest is deductible. However your combined mortgage debt is limited to that $1,000,000 ceiling.

Co-op owners may deduct the interest on any loan used to buy stock in the building, and their pro rata share of the interest on the master building mortgage, subject to the same limits as other homes. Additionally, though, the corporation itself must also fit within certain IRS requirements. Among other things, the building corporation must receive at least 80% of its income each year from the tenant-stockholders rather than from earnings on investments. You can read the details in IRS Publication 936 (Home Mortgage Interest Deduction). For more information on the mechanics and details of home ownership deductions in general, refer to IRS Publication 530 (Tax Information For First-Time Homeowners). You can download these from the Web, at **www.irs.gov/publications**, or by calling 800-TAX-FORM.

☑ How much money do you save with interest deductions?

Your tax savings will depend on how much interest you're going to pay, and what tax bracket you're in. Tax brackets change each year. They are based on your filing status (married, single, etc.) and your adjusted gross income level. The brackets are prorated, so even if you are in a higher tax bracket, part of your income is still taxed at the lower percentages.

Warning:

Some people believe if they're in the 28% tax bracket, making $120,000 per year, and if their mortgage interest deduction will be $24,000 per year, then they'll save 28% of $24,000, or $6,720.

This is not true. In reality, that number is too high, because of what's called *climbing the brackets*. If you make $120,000, then some if the income is taxed at 10%, some at 15%, some at 25% and only a very small amount—$50—at 28%. Your savings will be only $5,987.50.

Go to **www.irs.gov** to search on "tax schedules" for your current year. You can also obtain them from the post office or any accountant, or call the IRS, at 800-829-1040.

In addition, the IRS has an excellent tax calculator at **www.irs.gov/individuals/article/0,,id=96196,00.html**. You don't enter your name, they can't tell who you are, and all information is deleted as soon as you exit.

☑ Taxes due on a sale of your home

Under current tax laws, individuals may exclude up to $250,000 in gain from their taxes on a sale of their home if they lived in it as their principal residence for two of the prior five years. The years don't have to be consecutive. A married couple can exclude up to $500,000. That is the profit you can make without paying any income taxes if you also meet the requirements. There are limitations if you have a home office, if you rent out some portion to tenants, or if you've sold some excess land from the property. Obtain and read IRS Publication 523 (Selling Your Home), for more details.

$500,000 sounds like a lot of money, but you could make a larger profit than that. Or, the tax laws might change. Keep track of all the money you spend on improvements, as opposed to repairs. An *improvement* is something new that adds value, such as bathroom addition, intercom system, landscaping and sprinkler system, and other such things. Repairs, to maintain the status quo, don't help you out on your taxes. When you sell your home, the cost of all your improvements, plus the closing expenses that were added to basis, will decrease the size of your taxable profit.

Appendix D:
Checklists

For your convenience, the checklists found throughout this book have been repeated here. You can copy the ones you need and use them over and over again as you do your home buying.

Chapter 1: Deciding How Much Home You Can Afford
☑ **Examine how you spend your money now**
> ☑ Gather all your credit card statements for the last year
> ☑ Print out or collect all check registers for the past year
> ☑ Make a list of items you normally purchase with cash
> ☑ Calculate your average monthly take-home pay

☑ **Think about how your finances might change**
> ☑ What additional income can you count on?
> ☑ Will your net income decrease, and if so, by how much?
> ☑ How can you cut down on your expenses?
> ☑ Are you currently saving for a down payment?

☑ **Anticipate changes after a home purchase**
☑ **Prepare a housing budget**
☑ **Translate mortgage payment into maximum loan amount**
☑ **Improve your odds if finances are a problem**
> ☑ Search for rehap projects at below-market prices
> ☑ Shop for a duplex, small apartment building (four units), or something with a garage apartment
> ☑ Concentrate on foreclosure properties
> ☑ Limit your shopping to properties owned by sellers who will hold the financing
> ☑ Search for low-interest or no-interest rate loans for people who will buy homes in urban revitalization areas that your local government sponsors
> ☑ Talk to all of your friends, read everything you can read, and think creatively and expansively

Chapter 2: Credit Scores and Credit Repair
☑ **Obtain and improve your credit score**
  ☑ Find out target credit scores for lenders
  ☑ Order credit reports from all three agencies
  ☑ Beware of fraud
  ☑ Order and track your credit score
  ☑ Maintain good credit
  ☑ Improve your score

Chapter 3: Shopping for Financing

- ☑ Know your credit score
- ☑ Prepare a request for proposal
- ☑ Start collecting financial information about yourself
- ☑ Learn about special assistance programs
- ☑ Stay knowledgeable about expected rate changes
- ☑ Beware of add-on fees and discount points
- ☑ Plan ahead to avoid PMI charges
- ☑ Always ask if a seller will hold the financing

Chapter 4: Shopping for Insurance
- ☑ Obtain your C.L.U.E.® score and report
- ☑ Learn what influences your insurance premiums
- ☑ Choose several reputable companies for quotes
- ☑ Compare premiums and deductibles
- ☑ Compare coverages

Chapter 5: Deciding What Features You Want in a Home
- ☑ Location
- ☑ Price range
- ☑ Architectural style and age
- ☑ Property amenities
- ☑ Resale value
- ☑ What to do with your list of features

Chapter 6: Selecting a Real Estate Agent
- ☑ Understand the different real estate professionals
- ☑ Learn about particular specialties
- ☑ Determine what you want an agent to do
- ☑ Interview several people
- ☑ Sign a written contract with clear responsibilities

Chapter 7: Shopping For Sale By Owner (FSBO) Properties

☑ Prepare a questionnaire

☑ Learn about school zones

☑ Identify sources for FSBO information

☑ Research property values

☑ Make the most of your appointments

☑ Be ready to write your own contract and perform all follow-up

Chapter 8: Comparing Homes

- ☑ Determine what method of keeping track of information works for you
- ☑ Decide what information is important
- ☑ Read Chapter 14, "Comparing Land for Construction"
- ☑ Invest in a digital or disposable camera

Chapter 9: Comparing Condos

- ☑ Consider the age of the project
- ☑ Discover the personality of the community
- ☑ Weigh different restrictions
- ☑ Inventory common area features
- ☑ Calculate monthly dues
- ☑ Evaluate resale value

Chapter 10: Buying a Co-Op Apartment

☑ Compare all financial aspects of purchase and ownership

☑ Determine how difficult it is to obtain Board approval for purchase

☑ Find out if there is building security and full-time maintenance

☑ Identify potential lenders early

Chapter 11: Comparing New Manufactured Housing
- ☑ Know where the home will be installed
- ☑ Investigate the manufacturer's history and reputation
- ☑ Obtain copies of manufacturer's warranties
- ☑ Require unbundled quotes
- ☑ Recognize financing risks

Chapter 12: Comparing Houseboats
- ☑ Recognize financing difficulties
- ☑ Discuss docking requirements
- ☑ Anticipate differing needs for bodies of water

Chapter 13: Selecting Land on which to build

- ☑ Choose a location
- ☑ Consider topographic challenges
- ☑ Factor in existing vegetation
- ☑ Make sure utilities are available
- ☑ Think about the neighbors

Chapter 14: Comparing Land for Construction
- ☑ Distinguish between subdivisions and other land
- ☑ Find out if the current owner has a recent survey
- ☑ Learn about recreational and resort area restrictions
- ☑ Understand all about septic tanks, field lines, and perc tests
- ☑ Think about topographic considerations
- ☑ Consider unusual construction expenses

Chapter 15: Working with a Contractor or Construction Company

- ☑ Choose the right level of construction supervision
- ☑ Select three construction professionals to interview
- ☑ Do a background check
- ☑ Understand your lender's construction policies
- ☑ Manage the planning meeting
- ☑ Prepare a construction budget
- ☑ Understand change orders—a trap for the unwary
- ☑ Sign a contract
- ☑ Inspect what you expect

Chapter 16: Specifying Finishes and Fixtures in a New Home
- ☑ Determine if you can specify finishes and fixtures
- ☑ Obtain a budget and schedule from the builder
- ☑ Make wise choices
- ☑ Put your finish schedule in writing

Chapter 17: Preparing an Offer

- ☑ Find out if there is a widely used form contract in the community
- ☑ Remember—everything is negotiable
- ☑ Pay attention to seemingly unimportant details
- ☑ Spell out important monetary terms
- ☑ Specify exactly what you're buying and when
- ☑ Require the seller to provide you with certain documents before closing
- ☑ List circumstances that will allow you to cancel the contract without penalty
- ☑ Be specific about allocating closing expenses and prorates
- ☑ Prepare for the worst—what happens if someone defaults

Chapter 18: Hiring a Home Inspector
- ☑ Order property reports to assist your inspector
- ☑ Obtain the names of three inspectors to interview
- ☑ Do a phone interview and ask for sample reports
- ☑ Check scheduling, turnaround time, and fees
- ☑ Make your choice and be present during the inspection

Chapter 19: Clearing Contingencies

- ☑ Identify all contract contingencies and deadlines
- ☑ Note which ones depend on other people
- ☑ Make a schedule of reminders and deadlines
- ☑ Put everything in writing
- ☑ Send the right notices

Chapter 20: Seller Financing

☑ Put important terms in the real estate contract

☑ Include a contract contingency for loan document review

☑ Offer to write the note and the mortgage

☑ Deliver the note and mortgage to the closing company

Chapter 21: Cancelling a Contract

- ☑ Identify the contractual reason you are cancelling the contract
- ☑ Confirm the time limits within which you must give notice
- ☑ Make sure notice is given in the proper manner
- ☑ Obtain confirmation of the cancellation
- ☑ Obtain refund of earnest money

Chapter 22: Deciding How You Want to Hold Title
- ☑ Sole ownership in one person's name
- ☑ Tenants in common
- ☑ Joint tenants with right of survivorship
- ☑ Tenancy by the entireties
- ☑ Limited liability company
- ☑ Ask the title company about other ways to hold real estate

Chapter 23: Information to Give the Title or Escrow Company
☑ Title or escrow company
☑ Prior owner

Chapter 24: Finalizing Loan Arrangements

- ☑ Send out new requests for proposal
- ☑ Fill out an application and secure a written commitment
- ☑ Determine the expiration of any interest rate lock
- ☑ Complete loan-related requirements
- ☑ Obtain an estimated closing statement from the lender
- ☑ Make sure loan package and requirements are sent to the closing company

Chapter 25: Closing

- ☑ Make sure you have all documents necessary for closing
- ☑ Find out if you must bring certified funds
- ☑ Be prepared to ask questions
- ☑ Use this opportunity to obtain free advice

Chapter 26: Document Management
- ☑ Obtain a list of closing documents
- ☑ Request multiple copies of important paperwork
- ☑ File papers someplace you can find them again

Chapter 27: Preparing to Leave Your Rental Property

- ☑ Read your current lease
- ☑ Start a change of address box
- ☑ Make a list of all deposits and when they will be refunded
- ☑ Get rid of stuff BEFORE the move
- ☑ Ask if your landlord offer incentives if you find a replacement tenant
- ☑ Schedule a landlord walk-through inspection

Chapter 28: Moving

- ☑ **As soon as you start looking for a new home**
    - ☑ Create a moving box
    - ☑ Start a list of anyone who will need to know your new address
    - ☑ Set up a box for discards
    - ☑ Interview movers or price moving truck rentals
    - ☑ Find a source for inexpensive boxes
    - ☑ Confirm the expiration date

- ☑ **When you know you want to make an offer on a home**
    - ☑ Check schedules for movers or price moving truck rentals
    - ☑ Find out about self-storage availability
    - ☑ Talk to an insurance agent about moving insurance
    - ☑ Obtain a firm quote if using professional movers

- ☑ **After your offer is accepted and before closing**
    - ☑ Arrange for utility service shut-offs and turn-ons
    - ☑ Meet with an insurance agent for an insurance binder
    - ☑ Confirm movers
    - ☑ Schedule and conduct a walk-through with the sellers
    - ☑ Make reservations for house cleaning assistance
    - ☑ Find out the requirements at your children's new school and make sure everyone is familiar with the new neighborhood
    - ☑ Prepare all change of address notices
    - ☑ Send an introduction to your new neighbors
    - ☑ Begin packing
    - ☑ Buy colored tags and labels

- ☑ **Moving day**
    - ☑ Put all your important items in your moving box
    - ☑ Pack an ice chest
    - ☑ Move!

Index

About the Author

Denise L. Evans is the author of *How to Make Money on Foreclosures* and *How To Buy a Condominium or Townhouse.* She is a member of the Texas Bar Association, a licensed real estate broker, and an Adjunct Professor of Real Estate Studies at the University of Alabama College of Commerce and Business Administration. She is also a Research Associate for the Alabama Real Estate Research and Education Center, a candidate for the coveted CCIM (Certified Commercial Investment Member) designation, and a frequent speaker on real estate related topics for national and local audiences.

In her more than twenty years involved in real estate, as a homeowner, investor, developer, lender's attorney, closing attorney, broker, and consultant, she has been intimately involved with all aspects and sizes of transactions. From the creative financing to buy her first home—a $99,000 foreclosure—to representing lenders or borrowers in multimillion-dollar developments on the brink of foreclosure, she's had an opportunity to learn from the best in the country and to pass along their secrets and insights, along with her own, to readers of her books and articles.